ANCIENT EGYPTIAN HISTORY

OUTLINES OF
ANCIENT EGYPTIAN
HISTORY

By AUGUSTE MARIETTE

TRANSLATED AND EDITED, WITH NOTES, BY
MARY BRODRICK

SECOND EDITION

LONDON
JOHN MURRAY, ALBEMARLE STREET
1892

TRANSLATOR'S PREFACE

FOR some time past I have been asked, both in England and abroad, to recommend a short history of Ancient Egypt, to which my reply has invariably been—Mariette's ' Aperçu.' There is no history so concise or so comprehensive ; though, as its name says, it is but an outline.

To bring it within the reach of those who cannot, or who do not care to read it in the original, and so to make it better known to both the English and American public, has been my object in translating it. In doing so, I have endeavoured to give the entire sense of Mariette's words in readable English, rather than in an elaborate word-for-word translation. The book having been written in lecture form for the use of the Egyptian schools in Cairo, it will be found that here and there sentences, having particular reference to that fact, have been omitted or adapted : also that dates have been given according to our era, and not only as before or after the Hegira, which is, of course, the modern Egyptian mode of reckoning; while statements which are now proved to be false or doubtful have been omitted.

In some places, where the progress of events or fresh discoveries have made them necessary, notes have been added; and special notice of the finding of the royal mummies at Dêr-el-Bahari is also given.

I wish most gratefully to acknowledge the kindness of Mr. Le Page Renouf, Keeper of Egyptian and Assyrian Antiquities in the British Museum, who has read this work both in manuscript and proof, and has given me much help and many valuable suggestions. It must not, however, be supposed that this makes him in any way responsible for the opinions of the learned author.

M. BRODRICK.

PREFACE

TO

THE SECOND EDITION

THE kind reception accorded to this little book, together with the fact that the 'Aperçu' is now out of print, encourages me to venture on a Second Edition. To it has been added a sketch map of the Dynasties, a list of the principal Cartouches, a short notice of the Hyksos, an Index, and such notes and corrections as the progress of scientific research has rendered necessary.

M. B.

London, 1892.

CONTENTS

CHAPTER I

CHAPTER II

CHAPTER III

CHAPTER IV

CHAPTER V

CHAPTER VI

CHAPTER VII

PART II

APPENDIX

CHAPTER VIII

CHAPTER IX

Lake Mareotis · Lake Menzaleh · El Arish

SAIS DYN^S · XOIS DYN
XXVI. XXVIII. XIV.
MENDES DYN. XXIX.
DYN. XXX. SEBENNYTOS
SAN HYKSOS
DYN^S XXI. XXIII.
BUBASTIS DYN. XXII.
PITHOM

Natron
Lakes

ON
CAIRO

DYN^S IV. PYRAMIDS ▲ MEMPHIS
DYN^S IV. V. SAKKARAH · DYN^S III-V. VII. VIII.
DASHÛR ▲

El Fayûm
Lake Moeris

HERACLEOPOLIS
DYN^S IX. X.

BENI HASAN DYN. XII.
TELL-EL-AMARNA DYN. XVIII.

SIÛT

DYN^S I. II. THINIS
DYN^S XII. XIII. ABYDOS
KENEH
DENDERAH
DYN^S XI-XIII.
DYN^S XVIII-XX.
THEBES
Dêr-el-Bahari
KARNAK
LUXOR
Bab-el-Molûk
MEDINET HABÛ
ESNEH · EL KAB
EDFÛ

SILSILEH
KOM OMBOS

SKETCH MAP OF
DYNASTIES

DYN. VI. ELEPHANTINE · ASSÛAN
PHILAE

L.B.A.B. del.
Walker & Boutall sc.

TABLE OF THE PRINCIPAL KINGS OF ANCIENT EGYPT, WITH THEIR CARTOUCHES

DYNASTY I.—THINITE

			B.C.					B.C.
I		Mena . .	4400	5		Hesep-ti . .		4266
2		Teta . .	4366	6		Mer-ba-pen .		4233
3		Atet . .	4333	7		Semen-Ptah .		4200
4		Ata . . .	4300	8		Qebh . .		4166

DYNASTY II.—THINITE

			B.C.					B C.
9		Neter-baiu	. 4133	11		Ba-en-neter	.	4066
10		Ka-kau .	. 4100	12		Uat'-nes .	.	4033
		13	Senta.	. . 4000				

DYNASTY III.—MEMPHITE

14		T'at'ai .	. 3966	17		Teta	. . 3866
15		Neb-ka .	. 3933	18		Set'es	. . 3833
		Ser .	. . 3900	19		1 Nefer-ka-Ra 2 Huni	3800
		20	Sneferu	. . 3766			

DYNASTY IV.—MEMPHITE

		B.C.			B.C.
21	Khufu	3733	23	Khaf-Ra	3666
22	Tat-f-Ra	3700	24	Men-kau-Ra	3633

25 Shepses-ka-f . 3600

DYNASTY V.—ELEPHANTINÉ

26	User-ka-f.	3566	30	1 User-en-Ra 2 An	3433
27	Sahu-Ra	3533	31	Men-kau-Hor	3400
28	Kakaa	3500	32	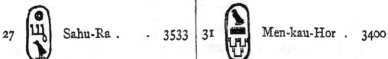 1 Tat-ka-Ra 2 Assa	3366
29	1 Nefer-f-Ra 2 Shepses-ka-Ra	3466	33	Unas	3333

DYNASTY VI.—MEMPHITE

			B.C.				B.C.
34		Teta	3300	38		Nefer-ka-Ra (Pepi II.) }	3166
35		1 User-ka-Ra 2 Ati }	3266	39		Mer-en-se(?)-em-sa-f }	3133
36		1 Meri-Ra 2 Pepi I. }	3233	40		Neter-ka-Ra	3100
37		1 Mer-en-Ra 2 Hor-em-sa-f }	3200	41		1 Men-ka-Ra 2 Nit-aqert } (*Queen Nitocris*)	3066

DYNASTIES VII.-XI.

			B.C.				B.C.
42		Nefer-ka-Ra	3033	45		Nefer-ka-Ra-khentu }	2933
43		Nefer-ka-Ra-nebi	3000	46		Mer-en-Hor	2900
44		Tat-ka-Ra-Maat	2966	47		Se-nefer-ka-Ra	2866

		B.C.				B.C.
48	Ka-en-Ra	. 2833	53	Nefer-kau-Ra	.	2666
49	Nefer-ka-Ra-terer	2800	54	Nefer-kau-Hor.		2600
50	Nefer-ka-Hor	. 2766	55	Nefer-ari-ka-Ra		2566
51	Nefer-ka-Ra-Pepi-senb }	2733	56	1 Neb-kher-Ra 2 Mentu-hotep (V.) }		2533
52	Nefer-ka-Ra-annu }	. 2700	57	Se-ankh-ka-Ra		2500

DYNASTY XII.—THEBAN

58	1 Se-hotep-ab-Ra 2 Amen-em-hat (I.) }	 2466
59	1 Kheper-ka-Ra 2 Usertsen (I.) }	 2433
60	1 Nub-kau-Ra 2 Amen-em-hat (II.) }	 2400

a

B.C.

61   1 Kha-kheper-Ra
     2 Usertsen (II.) · · · · · 2366

62   1 Kha-kau-Ra
     2 Usertsen (III.) · · · · · 2333

63   1 Maat-en-Ra
     2 Amen-em-hat (III.) · · · · 2300

64   1 Maat-kheru-Ra
     2 Amen-em-hat (IV.) · · · · 2266

A gap which comprises more than 500 years, and during which the time of the Hyksos falls. In all Dynasties XIII.–XVII., B.C. 2233–1733, circa.

DYNASTY XVIII.—THEBAN

65   1 Neb-peh-tet-Ra
     2 Aahmes (I.) (*Amosis or Amasis I.*) · · 1700

66   1 Ser-ka-Ra
     2 Amen-hotep (I.) · · · · · · 1666

67   1 Aa-kheper-ka-Ra
     2 Tehuti-mes (I.) · · · · · 1633

			B.C.
68		1 Aa-kheper-en-Ra 2 Tehuti-mes (II.) }	1600
69		1 Maat-ka-Ra 2 Hat-shepset-khnem-Amen. (*Queen Hatshepsu*) } .	—
70		1 Men-kheper-Ra 2 Tehuti-mes (III.) }	—
71		1 Aa-kheperu-Ra 2 Amen-hotep-neter-haq-Annu (II.) } .	1566
72		1 Men-kheperu-Ra 2 Tehuti-mes (IV.) }	1533
73		1 Maat-neb-Ra 2 Amen-hotep-haq-Uast. (*Amen-hotep III.*) }	1500
74		1 Nefer-kheperu-Ra-ua-en-Ra 2 Amen-hotep-haq-Uast 3 Khu-n-Aten. (*Amen-hotep IV.*) } .	1466

---

		1 Ser-kheperu-Ra-sotep-en-Ra 2 Amen-meri-en-Hor-em-heb. (*Horus*) } .	1433

One generation of heretic kings.

DYNASTY XIX.—THEBAN

B.C.

75
1 Men-pehtet-Ra
2 Ra-messu. (*Ramses I.*) } . . . 1400

76
1 Men-Maat-Ra
2 Amen-meri-en-Seti
3 Meri-en-Ptah. (*Seti I. Meneptah I.*) } 1366

77
1 User-Maat-Ra-sotep-en-Ra
2 Ra-messu-meri-Amen. (*Ramses II.*) } . 1333

78
1 Ba-en-Ra-meri-en-Amen
2 Ptah-meri-en-hotep-her-Maat. } . . 1300
   (*Meneptah II.*)

79
1 Khu-en-Ra-sotep-en-Ra
2 Ptah-meri-en-se-Ptah. (*Meneptah III.*) } . 1266

80
1 User-khau-Ra-meri-Amen
2 Ra-meri-Amen-merer-Set-nekht. } . . 1233
   (*Setnekht*)

DYNASTY XX.—THEBAN

81
1 User-Maat-Ra-meri-Amen
2 Ra-meses-haq Annu. (*Ramses III.*) } . 1200

B.C.

82   1 User-Ra-sotep-en-Amen
2 Ra-meses-meri-Amen-Ra-haq-Maat. } . 1166
(*Ramses IV.*)

83   1 User-Maat-Ra-sotep-en-kheper-Ra
2 Ra-mes-meri-Amen-Amen suten-f. } . —
(*Ramses V.*)

84   1 Ra-Amen-Maat-meri-neb
2 Ra-Amen-meses-neter Annu. (*Ramses VI.*)} —

85   1 Ra-user-Amen-meri-sotep-en-Ra
2 Ra-Amen-meses-ta-neter-haq-Annu. } . —
(*Ramses VII.*)

86   1 Ra-user-Maat-khu-en-Amen
2 Ra-Amen-meses-meri-Amen. (*Ramses VIII.*)} —

87   1 Se-kha-en-Ra Meri-Amen
2 Ra-meses-se-Ptah. (*Ramses IX.*) } . . —

88   1 Nefer-kau-Ra-sotep-en-Ra
2 Ra-meses-merer-Amen-kha-Uast. (?) } . —
(*Ramses X.*)

89   1 Ra-kheper-Maat-sotep-en-Ra
2 Ra-mes-suten Amen. (*Ramses XI.*)} . —

B.C.

90   1 User-Maat-Ra-sotep-nu-Ra
     2 Amen-mer-Ra-meses. (*Ramses XII.*) } · —

91   1 Men-Maat-Ra-sotep-en-Ra
     2 Ra-meses-merer-Amen-kha Uast neter
        haq Annu. (*Ramses XIII.*) } · 1133

Dynasty XXI.—THEBAN

92   1 Neter-hen-hotep-en-Amen
     2 Her-Hor-se-Amen. (*Her-Hor*) } · · 1100

93   Pai-net'em I.   .   .   .   .   —

94   1 Kheper-kha-Ra-sotep-en-Amen
     2 Amen-meri-Pai-net'em (II.) } · · —

Dynasty XXII.—BUBASTITE

95   1 Kheper-sekhet-Ra-sotep-en-Ra
     2 Amen-meri-Shashanq (I.) } · · 966

B.C.

96   1 Kherp-kheper-Ra-Sotep-en-Ra
      2 Amen-meri-Uasarken. (*Osorkon I.*)   . —

97   1 Het'-kheper-Ra-sotep-en-Ra
      2 Amen-Meri-Auset-meri-thakeleth.
         (*Takeleth I.*)   . —

98   1 User-Maat-Ra-sotep-en-Amen
      2 Amen-meri-Uasarken. (*Osorkon II.*)   . —

99   1 Kheper-sekhem-Ra-Sotep-en-Amen
      2 Amen-meri-Shash[anq] (II.)   . —

100   Takeleth II. . . . . —

101   1 User-Maat-Ra-sotep-en-Amen
      2 Amen-meri-se-Bast-Shashanq (III.)   . —

102   1 User-Maat-Ra-sotep-en-Amen
      2 Amen-meri-Pa-mai   . . —

103   1 Aa-kheper-Ra
      2 Shash[an]q IV. . . . . . —

DYNASTY XXIII.—TANITE

B.C.

104 Amen-meri-Peta-se-Bast 766

105 1 Aa-kheper-Ra-sotep-en-Amen
     2 Ra-Amen-meri-Uasarkena. (*Osorkon III.*) . —

DYNASTY XXIV.—SAÏTE

106 Bakenranf. (*Bocchoris*) 733

DYNASTY XXV.—ETHIOPIAN

107 Pa-ankhi. (*Piankhi*) . . . . . —

108 1 Nefer-ka-Ra
     2 Shabaka. (*Sabaco*) 700

109 1 Tat-kau-Ra
     2 Shabataka . . . . . —

110 1 Ra-nefer-tem-khu
     2 Taharaqa. (*Tirhakah*) . . . —

DYNASTY XXVI.—SAÏTE

B.C.

111   1 Uah-ab-Ra
     2 Psamthek. (*Psammetichus I.*) } . . . 666

112   1 Nem-ab-Ra
     2 Nekau. (*Necho*) } 612

113   1 Nefer-ab-Ra
     2 Psamthek. (*Psammetichus II.*) } . . 596

114   1 Haa-ab-Ra
     2 Uah-ab-Ra. (*Apries*) } 591

115   1 Khnem-ab-Ra
     2 Aahmes-se-Nit. (*Amasis II.*) } . . 572

116   1 Ankh-ka-en-Ra
     2 Psamthek. (*Psammetichus III.*) } . 528

DYNASTY XXVII.—PERSIAN

117   Kambathet. (*Cambyses*) 527

B.C.

118   Khshaiarsha. (*Xerxes the Great*)   .   .   . 486

119   Artakhshashas. (*Artaxerxes*)   465

120   1 Ra-meri-Amen
2 Antherirutsha. (*Darius Xerxes*)   .   . 521

DYNASTY XXVIII.—SAÏTE

121   Amen-rut. (*Amyrtæus*)   .   .   .   —

DYNASTY XXIX.—MENDESIAN

122   Niafaaurut 399

123   1 Khnem-Maat-Ra
2 Haker   393

124   1 User-Ra-sotep-en-Ptah ⎫
       2 Psamut   ⎭   380

B.C.

DYNASTY XXX.—SEBENNYTUS

125   1 S-net'em-ab-Ra-sotep-en-Amen ⎫
       2 Nekht-Hor-hebt-meri-Amen.   ⎬   .   . 378
          (*Nectanebo I.*)   ⎭

126   1 Kheper-ka-Ra   ⎫
       2 Nekht-neb-f.   (*Nectanebo II.*) ⎭   .   .   —

INTRODUCTION

HISTORY teaches that Egypt is bounded on the north by the Mediterranean Sea and on the south by the Cataract at Assûan; but history, in making these boundaries, ignores those lines of demarcation laid down by geography and ethnology.

To the north-east of the African continent, between the sea and the Equator, lies an immense strip of land formed by the river, and by it alone fertilized. Of the various races who inhabit the banks of this river some are rude savages, and incapable of self-government; while on this side of the tropics there is a nation which by its industry, fame, and capacity for civilization is the admiration of all. History ought to have said that where flowed the Nile there was Egypt; so that Egypt has the right to claim all land, however far south, which is watered by that famous river.

It is a country favoured above most. Within it dwells a people of gentle manners, kindly instincts, easy to teach, capable of progress; while cold and hunger, which, in less favoured lands become positive social evils, are warded off from it by the mildness of its climate and the fertility of the soil.   And what of the Nile itself?   It is the very king of rivers.   Year by year, almost to a given day, it rises, and, then swelled by the tropical rains that fall into it from the Sûdan, overflows the land on either side of its banks, leaving in its train a deposit of rich fertilizing mud.

In most countries an inundation is a public calamity, but in Egypt, so far is the annual overflow of the Nile from being regarded as a difficulty with which to cope, that it is hailed with delight.   It is the very wealth of Egypt.

The national history of the country is well worth study, for the part which Egypt has played in the world's history has been remarkable.   Equidistant from Europe, Asia, and Africa Proper, it may be said that no important event has ever taken place in which, by the very nature of things, she was not concerned.   It is, in fact, one of the salient points of her history.   Unlike so many countries, Egypt did not shine brilliantly for a time, only to sink into a period of greater or less darkness.   On the contrary, she had the unusual fortune of maintaining her influence through sixty-six centuries, and at nearly every epoch during that immense time proved herself a power not to be gainsaid.

It was Egypt who in the very earliest times appeared, under the Pharaohs, as the ancestor of all nations.   At the time when history was not, Cheops was raising monuments which modern art can never hope to surpass ; and from every one of the then known races of mankind, Thothmes, Amenophis, and Ramses were bringing home captives chained to their victorious chariot-wheels. In Greek and Roman times Egyptian thought preserved for the country that pre-eminence which aforetime was the result of valour ; and in that great mental struggle out of which issued the modern world it was the Alexandrian school of philosophy that in the supreme crisis led the way. In the Middle Ages it was Arab art that beautified Cairo ; at Mansûrah St. Louis lay a prisoner during the Crusades ; and in this century it was in Egypt that Buonaparte risked one of his most daring and brilliant campaigns ; and now, under the Mahomet-Ali dynasty, Egypt is seen re-civilizing herself, and by persistent efforts in the direction of progress forcing herself upon the notice of other nations. By her history, therefore, far more than from the fertility of her soil, does Egypt demand attention.

Plato relates that when Solon visited Egypt, the priests of Saïs [1] said to him, ' O Solon, Solon ! you Greeks, you are nothing but children ; there is not one old man among you in all Greece ! ' To have opened the way along which for 2,500 years so many nations have followed in her train is for all time Egypt's crowning glory.

The general history of Egypt, from its remotest period

[1] Sâ-el-Hâgar.

to our own times, may, roughly speaking, be divided into three periods—

     1. The Heathen Period.
     2. The Christian Period.
     3. The Mussulman Period.

During the Heathen Period, Egypt possessed—uninterruptedly—religion, writing, language, in fact, everything required to build up that civilization whose ruins may be found on either bank of the Nile.

It began with the monarchy, and, lasting through 5,385 years, came to an end when the Emperor Theodosius, in A.D. 381, proscribed the old national deities, and ordered that from henceforth Christianity should be the established religion of the country.

The Christian Period opened with the promulgation of the edict of Theodosius, and lasted until eighteen years after the Hegira,[2] when the officers of Mohammed forced the Mussulman religion upon Egypt.   During this time—only 259 years—the country was held by the Byzantine emperors, whose capital was at Constantinople.

The third period commenced with the establishment of Islamism, and is yet in existence.

This abstract of Egyptian history will embrace only the two first periods ; that is to say, from the beginning of history in Egypt until the day when Mohammedanism, brought in by the Arabs, took possession of the Nile country.

[2] A.D. 640.

OUTLINES

OF

ANCIENT EGYPTIAN HISTORY

CHAPTER I

HEATHEN PERIOD

THE numerous kings who in turn reigned upon the throne of Egypt are divided into families or dynasties, which, when native, took their titles from those towns chosen to be official seats of government : thus we have the dynasties of Memphis, Thebes, Elephantiné, and Tanis, according as the kings reigned either at Mitrahineh, Medinet Habû, Geziret-Assûan, or Sân. If, on the other hand, the dynasty was not native, but came in by conquest, it took the name of the conquering country; so that there were Ethiopian, Persian, Greek, and Roman dynasties. From the foundation of the Egyptian monarchy there were in all thirty-four. All the monuments, as in fact the *whole* history of the Heathen Period, are dated by the accession of the respective dynasties; each

B

dynasty corresponding to a royal or distinguished family inhabiting towns chosen by them, for the time being, as the capitals of Egypt.

Before entering upon the history of Egypt, we must take a rapid glance at the materials from which the Heathen Period is reconstructed. They come from three sources.

First and foremost in value and in quantity are the Egyptian monuments themselves : the temples, palaces, tombs, statues, and inscriptions. These have supreme authority, because they have the advantage of being the incontestable evidence of the events which they record. They have not long enjoyed this distinction, as the secret of the mysterious writing with which they are covered was, until lately, lost ; and it was difficult to see in these relics of antiquity anything more than lifeless stones, devoid of interest. But about sixty years ago there appeared, in the person of Champollion, a true genius, who succeeded, by his keen insight, in throwing the most unexpected light upon the darkness of the Egyptian script. Through him these old monuments, so long silent, caused their voices to be heard ; by him was the veil torn asunder, and the Egypt of bygone days, so renowned for her wisdom and power, stood revealed to the modern world. No longer are the monuments objects of hopeless curiosity, rather are they books of stone wherein may be read, in legible writing, the history of the nation with which they were contemporaneous.

Next to the monuments in importance comes the

Greek history of Egypt, written by Manetho, an Egyptian priest, about B.C. 250 ; and were the book itself in existence, we could have no more trustworthy guide. Egyptian by birth and priest by profession, Manetho, besides being instructed in all the mysteries of his religion, must have also been conversant with foreign literature, for he was a Greek scholar, and equal to the task of writing a complete history of his own country in that language. If only we had that book to-day it would be a priceless treasure ; but the work of the Egyptian priest perished, along with many others, in the great wreck of ancient literature,[1] and all we possess of it are a few fragments preserved in the pages of subsequent historians.

After Manetho and the monuments, though occupying but quite a secondary place, is the information acquired second-hand through the Greek and Latin authors. First there is Herodotus,[2] who visited Egypt B.C. 450, and who has given a vivid description of the country ; then later on, about B.C. 8, Diodorus Siculus,[3] a Greek traveller, wandered up and down the banks of the Nile and, like Herodotus, devoted a special chapter of his book to Egypt. But the most accurate as well as useful account of Egypt is that furnished by Strabo,[4] a Greek geographer contemporary with Diodorus. Lastly, in A.D. 90, Plutarch wrote his celebrated treatise in Greek entitled ' De Iside et Osiride,' a work which the

---

[1] Burning of the library at Alexandria.
[2] Book II.
[3] Book I.
[4] Book XVII.

discoveries of modern science are every day proving to be a faithful echo of the traditions of Ancient Egypt.

Having made these preliminary remarks in order to show upon what grounds we shall base this sketch of Ancient Egyptian history, we will proceed to divide the Thirty-four Dynasties into five great epochs :

The Ancient Empire.	Dynasties	I.—XI.
The Middle Empire.	„	XI.—XVIII.
The New Empire.	„	XVIII.—XXXI.
Egypt under the Greeks.	„	XXXII.—XXXIII.
Egypt under the Romans.	„	XXXIV.

And we will begin with the Ancient Empire, the history of Egypt during the Heathen Period.

CHAPTER II

HEATHEN PERIOD—THE ANCIENT EMPIRE—
DYNASTIES I.—XI.

THE Ancient Empire begins with the foundation of the
Egyptian monarchy, about B.C. 5004, and ends with the
Eleventh Dynasty : it lasted 1,940 years. So far remote,
however, is the time when Egypt became a settled kingdom, that its early history seems enveloped in darkness.
This much, however—owing to the progress of science
generally and philology in particular—we do know, and
that is, that its prehistoric civilization, far from coming
from the south and following the course of the Nile,
migrated into the country from Asia ; though at what
far-away date the race now living on Egyptian soil appeared there, or what combination of circumstances
tended to develop their marvellous career, must ever
remain a problem. Whatever may prove its solution, on
this one point the authorities all agree. Mena was the
first authentic king of Egypt. Was he, as some say, the
successor of small territorial princes? Or was he the
first of them to unite the whole country under one rule ?
The absence of documents forbids an answer. But we

are sure that Mena was no legendary being, though the personality of the founder of the Ancient Egyptian Empire looms through a past so distant as to make him seem to belong to quite the early days of the human race.

According to Manetho, the first three dynasties reigned 769 years. They have left but few monuments to record their history ; and these are marked by a rudeness and indecision of style which suppose that as yet Egyptian art was in its infancy. Those dynasties, therefore, represent that primary period of development through which all peoples pass before they become a nation.

With the Fourth Dynasty, B.C. 4235, Egypt emerges from the obscurity with which it has hitherto been surrounded, and we are enabled to date facts by the help of the monuments. Chief among the kings of this period is the Cheops of Herodotus, the Khufu of contemporary texts. He seems to have been a warrior-king, for there are bas-reliefs at Wady Magharah.[1] which represent him as chastising the On, the Bedâwin of that day, who were annoying the eastern frontiers of Lower Egypt. But more than a soldier he was a builder, and the greatest and most remarkable of the Egyptian pyramids is his tomb. One hundred thousand men, who were relieved every three months, are said to have been employed for thirty years upon this gigantic undertaking. It would assuredly tax our modern ingenuity to be obliged to

[1] In the Sinaitic Peninsula.

construct a like monument ; but a far more difficult problem would be the erection within it of chambers and corridors which—notwithstanding the superincumbent weight of thousands of tons—should last perfectly unmoved for sixty centuries.[2] The Fourth Dynasty is the culminating point in the history of the Ancient Empire. By an extraordinary impulse, Egypt threw off all trammels and emerged in the glory of a fully developed civilization. From this moment class distinctions were recognised in

[2] The present height of the Great Pyramid is 451 feet ; in Abd-el-Latif's time it measured 477 ft. 3 in. ; and Diodorus gives its height in his day as about 480 ft. Originally it was 482 feet high, including the casing, so that it has lost about 31 feet since its erection. The square area of the Great Pyramid is, in round numbers, 13 acres, or about the size of Lincoln's Inn Fields. It was built of limestone, brought from the Mokattam Hills and from Tûrah, and of granite from Syene ; the casing was probably of the finest limestone.

Herodotus says : 'About 100,000 men were employed annually in each of these tasks (quarrying stones in the Arabian hills and transporting them to the Nile ; ferrying the blocks across the river, and conveying them from the river to the base of the Libyan Hills). They took ten years to make the road for the transport of the stones, which, in my opinion, must have been almost as laborious a task as the building of the pyramid itself, for the length of the road amounts to 3,051 feet, its breadth is 10 feet, its height at the highest place is 48 feet. It is constructed entirely of polished stone with figures engraven upon it. Ten years were consumed in making this road and the subterranean chambers on the hill, which the king caused to be excavated as his burial place. . . . Now the construction of the pyramid occupied twenty years. It is covered with polished stones, well jointed, none of which is less than thirty feet long.'

Egyptian society, and Art attained a breadth and dignity that even in later and more brilliant days were hardly surpassed. Towns were built ; large farms were established, on which thousands of heads of cattle were reared, and where antelopes, storks, and wild geese were domesticated. Abundant harvests repaid the careful cultivation of the soil. The architecture of the houses was good ; and there the master lived beloved and respected by his own people, spending his time in the cultivation of flowers, in hunting, in fishing in the numberless canals by which the country is intersected, and in watching the games and dances performed for his amusement ; and it was for him, too, that the great square-rigged boats journeyed up and down the Nile, representing what was doubtless a most thriving commerce. The infantine country seems at this point to have everywhere developed into a youth full of life and vigour. That splendid statue of Khafra, now in the Gizeh Palace, is, notwithstanding its six thousand years, a work of the finest execution. It is the production of the Fourth Dynasty. So too are the Pyramids, which from the very earliest times have been reckoned among the seven wonders of the world.

Under the first four dynasties, Thinis and Memphis were in turn selected as the capitals of Egypt ; but when the Fifth came in, the government was removed to Elephantiné. The kings of this dynasty did not distinguish themselves by any historically remarkable deeds, though they built several monuments worthy of record ;

amongst them are the Mastabat-el-Farûn [3] and several tombs in the necropolis of Sakkarah. At the death of the last king of the Fifth Dynasty,[4] a new family succeeded to the throne : and according to Manetho, they came from Memphis. Among their most celebrated members were Queen Nitocris and Apappus.[5] The former, 'the beauty with rosy cheeks,' as Manetho describes her, was the most remarkable woman of her time. Feeling called upon to avenge the death of her brother, who had been assassinated, she inveigled the murderers into a subterranean gallery, into which, during a feast which she had prepared for them, she secretly caused the waters of the Nile to flow and drown them all. Apappus, like Khufu, was a warrior. In his days the cataracts did not offer the same obstructions as they do now, and the southern frontier of Egypt was consequently exposed to the incursions of the Ua-ua, a restless negro population whom the king reduced to submission. A hitherto unknown tribe of Bedâwin, called the Herusha, was also subdued by the Egyptian forces ; while to the north, a hostile people who had made raids upon the copper-miners in the Sinaitic Peninsula received severe chastisement. At Assûan, at El-Kab, at Kasr-es-Syad, at Shêkh Saïd, at Zawit-el-Mytin, at Sakkarah, and at Sân,[6] the name of Apappus frequently appears :

---

[3] The Mastabat-el-Farûn was opened in 1882, and proved to be the pyramid of Unas. (Dyn. V.).

[4] Unas.

[5] Pepi II.

[6] Tanis, the Zoan of the Bible (Ps. lxxviii. 12).

and it may also be seen sculptured on the rocks at Wady Magharah, and at Hammamât, a station on the road between Keneh and Kossêr. The name Apappus signifies, in Egyptian, a giant, and this may be the basis of a tradition which describes him as being nine cubits high ; and also says that he reigned a hundred years.

From the end of the Sixth to the beginning of the Eleventh Dynasty, a period of nearly 436 years, the monuments are almost silent. The country was during this time overrun by a people as yet unknown to history, and of whom Manetho takes no account, as he mentions only the legitimate kings then shut up within their capitals. From a military point of view the invasion of Egypt presents no difficulty, as by its geographical position as well as from the richness of its internal resources it has ever been a point of attraction, and it is both its misfortune and its glory to have always been coveted of other nations. It would be too daring to assert without proof that the complete silence of the monuments is due to one of those crises which come in the history of nations as well as in the lives of men. May it not be that we are ignorant of the whereabouts of the monuments of those dynasties ? This is, however, a problem that can only be solved by means of excavations.

And so, after lasting nineteen centuries, the Ancient Empire closes. At this point the condition of Egypt is well worth attention. While as yet the world in general was plunged in the depths of barbarism ; and the nations that later on were to play so important a part in the world's history were still savages, the banks of the Nile were nurturing a people both cultivated and civilized ; and a powerful monarchy, aided by a complete organization of court functionaries and civil servants, was already ruling the fate of the nation. However far into the dim past we gaze, we are everywhere met by a fully developed civilization to which the succeeding centuries, numerous as they are, have added nothing. On the contrary, Egypt lost rather than gained ; for at no later period could she have raised such monuments as the Pyramids.

CHAPTER III

WITH the Eleventh Dynasty, B.C. 3064, began the Middle Empire, and after lasting for 1,361 years, it came to an end with the Eighteenth.

After the reigns of Apappus and Nitocris, which closed the Sixth Dynasty, a sudden and unforeseen check was given to the progress of civilization ; and during 436 years—from the Sixth to the Eleventh Dynasty— Egypt seems to have disappeared from the list of nations. When she awoke from her long sleep, on the accession of the Entefs and Mentuhoteps,[1] it was to find that her ancient traditions were quite forgotten. The old family names, the titles of the functionaries, the writing and even the religion itself, seemed new. No longer were Thinis, Elephantiné, and Memphis the capitals ; but Thebes was for the first time chosen as the seat of sovereign power. Besides this, Egypt had been shorn of a considerable portion of her territory, and the authority of her kings was limited to the Thebaïd. The monu-

---

[1] Dynasty XI.

ments, which are barbaric, primitive, sometimes even coarse, confirm all this ; and on looking at them, we might easily believe that Egypt under the Eleventh Dynasty had reverted to that period of infancy through which she had already passed under the Third.

Following upon the obscure kings of this royal family come the Usertsens, and Amen-em-hats, the powerful monarchs of the Twelfth Dynasty, and with them comes in one of the most brilliant epochs of Egyptian history.

In the time of Usertsen I., Egypt had for her northern boundaries the Mediterranean Sea and the Sinaitic Peninsula—her natural frontiers.   On the south she was already struggling for that large dominion which afterwards became hers for thirty centuries ; and the possession of which urged her to claim as her patrimony all countries watered by the Nile.   At this period the land of Cush, or Ethiopia, lay between the First Cataract and the south of Abyssinia, and was to Ancient Egypt what the Sûdan is to modern.   With varying boundaries, and without unity of organization, Ethiopia was the home of an enormous population, diverse in origin and race, but the bulk of whom were Cushites, a people of Hamitic descent, who, at some unknown period of history, had crossed the Straits of Bab-el-Mandeb, and seized upon Upper Egypt.   Under the Twelfth Dynasty, these Cushites were Egypt's bitterest foes, so that it was against the Sûdan that the forces of the nation were spent.   It was as a barrier against them that the fortresses of Kumneh and Semneh, on either bank of the Nile, were raised. They are beyond the Second Cataract, and marked the southern limit of the then Empire of the Pharaohs.

With the politics of the outside world the kings of the Twelfth Dynasty did not trouble themselves : they were content to remain at home within reach of their sacred river. During those struggles abroad which have made the names of the Usertsens and Amen-em-hats for ever famous, Egypt strengthened herself at home by a vigorous advance which made itself felt in all branches of civilization. A few isolated pyramids and the obelisk of Matarîyeh,[2] near Cairo, are all that is left to us whereby to judge of the buildings of this period ; for a foreign force which later on invaded the land entirely swept away all the magnificent edifices raised by the Twelfth Dynasty. But failing temples and palaces, we shall find in the unique hypogea of Beni-Haṣan the proof of what has just been stated ; and the thousand-and-one details reproduced on these tomb walls prove that under the rule of this dynasty Egypt enjoyed a period of greater prosperity than even under the Fourth. To take one of

[2] This obelisk stands on the site of the ancient city of An— the *On* of Genesis, the *Aven* of Ezekiel, the *Beth-Shemesh* of Jeremiah. It is made of red granite, brought from the quarries of Syene (Assûan), and is carved on all four sides with bold, clean-cut hieroglyphs, now becoming rapidly defaced by the wild bees, who have made their nests in them. It was erected by Kheper-ka-Ra (Usertsen I.), and must have been standing when Abram was first driven by famine to seek 'corn' in Egypt.'

these tombs in particular, that of Ameni, sometime general and mudîr of the province in which Beni-Hasan is situated.[8] There the every day life of Twelfth Dynasty Egypt is vividly portrayed. On one side we see depicted the fattening of cattle ; the ploughing up of the land with implements of the same kind as those used in Egypt to-day ; the reaping of corn, and the thrashing of it by animals who are treading out the sheaves with their feet. On the other side may be seen the navigation of the river ; the building and lading of large boats ; the making of beautiful furniture from valuable wood ; the manufacture of clothing. In a corner of the tomb Ameni recounts the story of his life : as general, he was sent into the Sûdan on a campaign, where he commanded a caravan of four hundred soldiers, charged with bringing gold from the mines of Gebel-Atoki to Coptos : as mudîr, he was commended by his sovereign for his wise administration of the province. 'All the lands from north to south,' he says, 'were ploughed and sown. Nothing was stolen from the magazines ; no child was grieved through me, nor any widow oppressed. I gave alike to the widow and the married woman, and never in any of my judgments did I prefer the great before the humble.' A further example and one of great importance will serve to show the strength of Egypt's internal resources under the Amen-em-hats and Usertsens. I mean Lake Mœris. We know what the Nile is to Egypt. If the periodical rise of its waters be insufficient, then part of the land is

[8] Minieh.

not inundated, and must remain barren. On the other hand, should the rise of its waters be excessive, the dikes are swept away, and whole villages are submerged, so that the land that should be fertilized is destroyed. Egypt is therefore perpetually threatened with two equally formidable misfortunes. In the face of such possible catastrophes, Amen-em-hat III., a king of the Twelfth Dynasty, conceived and put into execution a truly gigantic project. Buried in the desert on the western side of Egypt, there lies an oasis of cultivated land,[4] which is connected by a sort of isthmus with the country watered by the Nile. Towards the centre of this oasis stretches a large plateau whose general level is that of the Egyptian plains ; on the west lies a natural lake more than thirty miles long.[5] It was in the centre of this plateau that Amen-em-hat undertook to excavate an artificial lake that should cover a surface of ten million square metres.[6] Should the overflow of the Nile be in-sufficient, the water was brought into this lake and stored up, so to speak, for the irrigation not only of the Fayûm but of the whole left bank of the river as far as the sea. Did too high an inundation threaten the dikes, then the great reservoirs of the artificial lake were to be opened, and when its waters in their turn overflowed, the overflow was let out by a flood-gate into the Birket-el-Kurûn. The two names which the Egyptians gave to this won-derful work of Amen-em-hat III. have both become

---

[4] Fayûm.   [5] The Birket-el-Kurûn.
[6] Nearly four square miles.

historical. From one *Meri*, that is to say, the lake *par excellence*, the Greeks drew their tradition of a king bearing that name ; while the other, *P-iûm*—an old word meaning the sea—has become in the mouths of modern Arabs the appellation of a whole district owing its fertility to the endowment of a Twelfth Dynasty king.[7]

[7] The Fayûm. It is possible for the traveller to visit the site of Lake Mœris, the very existence of which it has been the fashion of late years to deny. So early as the days of Diodorus the lock gates, near the modern El-Lahûn, had fallen into decay, and the lake, going from bad to worse, had been so far lost as to cause doubts as to the reality of Herodotus' description of it. Professor Heinrich Brugsch, who spent some time this year in prosecuting scientific researches in the Fayûm, expresses a most emphatic opinion that there was abundant monumental evidence to show that at a very early period of Egyptian history there existed near the plateau of Hawâra an immense basin of water, which gave its name to a whole province, the Fayûm or 'lake district.' In ancient times there were forty-two divisions or nomes of Egypt, each having its own capital, local government, and *cultus*, and all more or less worshipping Osiris ; but from these it is evident the Fayûm was excluded. It formed an isolated part of the kingdom, was divided like the parent country into nomes with their governors, and, save in the necropolis at Hawâra, was given over to the worship of Sebek, the crocodile god. It was known in the hieroglyphs as Ta She, the lake district, which in Coptic became P-iûm, the maritime district, and survives to-day in the Arabic Fayûm. It is evident from the celebrated Fayûm papyrus, of which there are two copies, that the term Mer-uer, the great water, or lake, was also applied to it ; and perhaps herein lies the origin of the name 'Mœris.' The waters of this lake must have reached to the plateau of Hawâra, the necropolis of the inhabitants of a town called Shed, on the site of which stands the modern city of Medinet-el-Fayûm. It was in ancient times a royal residence, and contained a magnificent temple, dedicated to Sebek,

This alone gives an interest to the Usertsen family which may be said to be one of the most illustrious that ever occupied the throne of Mena : their reigns are to the Middle Empire what those of Khufu and Khafra were to the Ancient.

Information respecting the Thirteenth Dynasty, in which the Nefer-hoteps and Sebek-hoteps were preeminent, is furnished by the monuments only. Manetho gives no names, although he allows the dynasty a complement of sixty kings, whose successive reigns amount to 463 years. No building of this period has survived, though from the statues and stelæ found at Sân [8] and at Abydos, it may be gathered that Egypt had lost nothing of her former prosperity. The monuments being silent,

whose dimensions far exceeded those of the temples at Thebes. Tradition gives Amen-em-hat III. of the Twelfth Dynasty as the constructor of Lake Mœris, and his burial place is the crude-brick pyramid at Hawâra; but fragments bearing the cartouches of Amen-em-hat I. and Usertsen II., found near Medinet, would prove it of more ancient date. Moreover, it was hardly possible that a town of such dimensions as Shed would be built at any distance from water. A canal named Hune, or Hunet, cut from the Nile, fed the lake and provided for the needs of the city ; the mouth of it was called in the hieroglyphs La Hune, 'the opening of the canal,' a name which survives in the modern ' El-Lahûn.' There is an interesting allusion to this ' opening of the canal ' in the celebrated Stela of Piankhi, written about the eighth century B.C. Professor Brugsch has also most ingeniously suggested that Ra-pa-ro-hunet, ' the temple of the mouth of the canal,' might give us the derivation of the word ' labyrinth.' It must be remembered that in the hieroglyphs *l* and *r* are interchangeable letters.

[8] In the Delta.

we can only conjecture about the wars undertaken by these kings. From the excavations at Sân, and the finding of a Thirteenth Dynasty colossus on an island near to Dongola,[9] it may be concluded that they extended the frontiers laid down by the Twelfth Dynasty. There are, above Wady Halfah, near the village of Semneh, some rocks rising perpendicularly from the river, and upon them, twenty-two feet above the present high-water mark, are engraved some hieroglyphic inscriptions recording that in the Twelfth and Thirteenth Dynasties, the Nile at its highest reached the spot where these lines were traced. So that, forty centuries ago, the river at the cataract was nearly twenty-two feet higher than it is to-day. The reason for this is one of those problems which as yet science has been unable to elucidate. Was the alteration of the river bed at the Second Cataract due to one of those great hydrographical enterprises undertaken by the Middle Empire kings, and if so, was it done with the idea of regulating the impetuous rush of the inundation? Or may it have been that by rendering the cataract impassable to vessels coming from the Sûdan, they hoped to raise a natural barrier against Egypt's deadliest foes? No one can say.

Of the Fourteenth Dynasty we know absolutely nothing. According to modern authorities, it ruled in Lower Egypt while the Thirteenth held sway in Upper. But with this assertion some statues of the Thirteenth Dynasty kings found at Sân, and now in the Gizeh Palace,

[9] Argo.

do not agree : and it is not likely that if the kings of the Thirteenth Dynasty had been relegated to Upper Egypt, they would have beautified the temples placed under the protection of their rivals with their own portraits. Eusebius, who abridged Manetho, says that the two following dynasties (XVth and XVIth) came from Thebes, and while these royalties made the city of the Entefs [1] the capital of their empire, Northern Egypt became the scene of one of the most terrible misfortunes ever chronicled in the national history. Under the last kings of the Fourteenth Dynasty, the work of civilization continued, and the country was presumably walking in the paths of progress ; when suddenly, the Asiatic frontier of the Delta was invaded by a barbarous people to whom Manetho gives the appellation of Hyksos, or Shepherds. They massacred the people, pillaged the temples, and imposed their authority upon the northern provinces of Egypt by fire and sword. During four centuries the kings, banished into the Thebaïd, had for their neighbours, and probably for their masters, these barbarous hordes. To say what was the condition of Egypt during that time is impossible ; for there is not one monument of that miserable period left to tell us what became of the country's ancient glory under Hyksos rule. The vigorous impulse given to civilization by Usertsen was suddenly brought to a standstill, and the true sequence of the monuments interrupted, and we gather from this very silence how bitterly the country was suffering.

[1] Thebes.

The Seventeenth Dynasty can only be thoroughly studied by means of the monuments at the Gizeh Palace, and from them we learn that the kingdom then, as under the two preceding dynasties, was still divided between rival sovereigns. However, better days were at hand. The excavations in Upper Egypt, which have proved so barren of all information concerning the Fifteenth and Sixteenth Dynasties, have brought to light much concerning the Seventeenth. In the tombs at Gûrnah have been found the remains of a whole array of court functionaries, which proves the existence of a thoroughly civilized state. In Lower Egypt there arose a fresh dynasty of the Hyksos,[2] an off-shoot of the Khetas who inhabited the plains near the Taurus Mountains, and were worshippers of Sutekh. But they were not the iconoclasts that Manetho depicted ; on the contrary, the monuments prove that these conquerors of Egypt were themselves conquered by the civilization of the nation they had vanquished : and that Egypt by her art, her religion, and her inherent greatness, re-acted, so to speak, upon her oppressors.

To such an extent was this the case that while adorning the temple at Sân with their own portraits, they embodied them in Egyptian Sphinxes : they also adopted the writing of the country ; and little by little became Egyptians—real Pharaohs—calling themselves, as did her monarchs, 'Sons of the Sun.' It is true that these Hyksos honoured Sân as the abode of their god Sutekh,

[2] Having Sân (Tanis) for one of their strongholds.

thus making him their tutelary deity, but they never disturbed or proscribed the worship of the Egyptian gods, whom they equally with Sutekh adored, showing that, although they nominally had become Egyptians, they yet remained faithful to the god of their forefathers. A better state of things was ushered in by these new Hyksos, whose names both Manetho and the monuments have handed down to posterity as being far from hateful. Four centuries later we even find Ramses II., one of the great warrior kings, concluding a treaty of peace with the Khetas by celebrating at Sân the fourth secular anniversary of the accession of the Seventeenth Dynasty : and he on that occasion spoke, by courtesy, of Saïtes, its first king, as the ancestor of his race. In the south, as well as north, alike under the native kings and the Asiatic conquerors, Egypt seemed recovering from the long stupor into which she had fallen, and along the banks of the Nile arose a series of monuments, which, though bearing evident indications of the subjugation of the country, yet showed that the times were less troubled.

Although Ramses II., 400 years after the Hyksos rule, rebuilt Sân,[3] the city of Sutekh, and there paid homage

---

[3] Sân, or Tanis, the T'ân, or Zoan of the Bible, is situated about twenty miles north of Tell-el-Kebir. It is of extremely ancient date, the cartouche of Pepi I., a king of the Sixth Dynasty, having been discovered there. It is mentioned in the Old Testament as having been founded seven years later than Hebron. It was used by the Hyksos as their capital, and was probably the residence of Joseph. In the reign of Ramses II. it

to the Shepherd king who first brought the worship of that deity into Egypt, it must not be thought that the native princes exiled into the Thebaïd treated their rivals with the same consideration. A short but desperate war broke out, followed by the complete overthrow of the foreigners.[4] Driven into their capital, and there besieged

was celebrated for its beauty, for the fertility of its fields, and for the abundance of both wild birds and fish. 'He rejoices who has settled there.' Later on the priests of Zoan-Tanis sided with Her-Hor, the priestly usurper of the throne of Ramses. Under the Twenty-third Dynasty it was again the seat of government. In the stela of Piankhi on Gebel-Barkal we find an unnamed satrap ruling in Tanis. Finally, Assurbanipal subdued the city and took the governor prisoner.

For more complete descriptions of Tanis, see vols. ii. and v. of Egypt Exploration Fund Memoirs, and also the 'Letter of Panbesa' from the Anastasi Papyrus, in 'Records of the Past,' vol. vi. p. 11 *et seq.*

[4] The first to rise against the Hyksos was Sekenen-Ra, then only a 'haq,' or prince, 'in the city of the South.' It seems that Apepi, who had introduced the worship of Set or Sutekh into the Delta, sent an imperious message to Sekenen-Ra, desiring him to give up the worship of Amen-Ra, and pay homage to the new divinity alone. This the latter stoutly refused to do, and prepared for war. Sekenen-Ra fell fighting, in the endeavour to oust the Hyksos from Sân. His mummy was found amongst the collection at Dêr-el-Bahari, and, in consequence of the bad condition it was in, was opened in 1886 by M. Maspero, then Director-General of the Bûlaq Museum. It is the body of a man about six feet in height and well developed. There is a dagger wound across the right temple just above the eye, while a blow, probably from a hatchet or mace, or some such blunt instrument, has split the left cheek bone and broken the lower jaw. Beneath the hair is a long cleft caused by a splinter of the skull having been fractured off with a downward stroke from an axe. The Egyptians were

by the illustrious Aahmes or Amosis, the Asiatics were at last routed, and the majority of them, crossing the Isthmus, fled into Asia. The rest were permitted by Amosis to remain and cultivate the ground that their ancestors had seized. So closed this most disastrous page of Egyptian history, and by the victories of Amosis the old sceptre of Mena returned into the hands of its rightful owners. Once well out of the country they had usurped, the Hyksos never reappeared there, and when Egypt again met them, it was on the battle-field where they were mingled with the Khetas.

As for those whom the policy of Amosis retained on Egyptian soil, they formed in the eastern part of the Delta a little colony of foreigners tolerated there on the same grounds as were the Israelites—only that they had no Exodus—and by a curious fate we, to-day, meet these foreigners with their strong limbs and long severe faces, in the people living on the banks of Lake Menzaleh. Nor must it be forgotten that there is the strongest presumption for believing that the patriarch Joseph came into Egypt under the Shepherds, and that the scene of the touching story related in Genesis was laid at the court of one of these foreign kings. It must have been a Semite—like himself—whom Joseph served; and the elevation of a Hebrew to the dignity of prime minister is

probably victorious, though the loss of their brave soldier-king made it a dearly bought success; had they not been, they could not have rescued the body, and taken it to Thebes to be embalmed and buried.

the more easily explained if it occurred under a sovereign of kindred race.[5]

[Of the Hyksos, their nationality and their history in Egypt, we know very little, but owing to the recent researches of scholars we are able now to gather a few facts concerning them. The tradition of the *classic authors* was that the general name of the invaders was Hyksōs ('hyk' signified a king, and 'sōs' a shepherd, thus 'shepherd kings'); while Josephus states that 'it is mentioned in another work' that 'hyk' means prisoner. They apparently took possession of the land suddenly and with ease; treated the inhabitants with great cruelty, forbad the worship of the gods, and destroyed the temples. From among themselves they chose out one Salatis to be their king, who fortified the eastern frontier, repaired Avaris, and made it a stronghold with a garrison of 240,000 soldiers. He established himself at Memphis, and, after reigning nineteen years, died. Beon succeeded him, then followed Apachnas, Apōphis, Ianias, and Assis as the founders of the line. To the foreign dominion is given a duration of about 500 years.

From the *Monuments* we gather that during the obscure period immediately following upon the Thirteenth Dynasty the country was invaded by barbarians. They are never mentioned as Hyksos, but are called the Shasu 'shepherds or nomads;' the 'Aamu,' who 'were in the midst of Egypt of the north, and in the city of Hauar' (Avaris); the 'Asiatic nomads or shepherds,' the 'Aamu

[5] Probably Apepi.

of the East,' the 'plague' and the 'pestilence.' The specific country from which they came is never recorded. It is thus quite clear that they were vagrants—a wandering horde probably of mixed nationality, who took possession of the Delta and overran Egypt as far as the Fayûm.

It is not unlikely that they were a race, partly Semitic partly Turanian, who were pushed out, as it were, into Egypt from Western Asia. If we look at the history of Chaldæa, we shall find that country to have been the meeting-place of many races, their battle-ground, and in some cases their ultimate home. Is it possible that in one of the great uprisings such as we know took place these wanderers may have been forcibly ejected from the land they temporarily occupied? Syria, then divided up amongst wild tribes, and also intersected with Kheta fortified towns and liable as well to famines, was not likely to form a permanent halting-place, while the fertile Nile Valley offered every inducement as a settlement.

It is also evident from the Monuments that these nomads were strongly influenced by the civilization of the Egyptians. Doubtless their arrival was signalised by many acts of brutality, but they appear when settled to have adopted the ways and even the dress of the conquered people, at the same time strictly maintaining the worship of Sutekh, their own particular divinity. The Sallier papyrus, whether historical or legendary, clearly shows this.

The discoveries of Mariette at Tanis, a Hyksos town, brought to light two statues of an Egyptian king bearing a cartouche on the arm, which M. Naville reads as follows: ' The good god Ra-aa-Kenen, the son of Ra-Apepi.' This is a clear case of a statue of a native predecessor being appropriated by a Hyksos ruler, who, though a worshipper of Sutekh, yet called himself a son of Ra. From the mathematical papyrus in the British Museum we learn the name of another of these princes, Ra-aa-User, with the coronation name of Apepi ; and a broken statue found by M. Naville at Bubastis bearing the name User en Ra Ian-Ra is, both from the workmanship and the inscription, judged to be that of a Hyksos ruler. The pose and detail of this and two other kindred statues are entirely Egyptian, while the character of the faces is Turanian.

Professor Virchow, the great German ethnologist, seeing the celebrated Hyksos head from Bubastis in the British Museum, at once pointed out its foreign features, and, while saying how difficult it would be to strictly define the nationality, thought that it might be that ' the models of these heads were Turanians, but I should not be able to say which.' Professor Flower inclines to the view of the Mongoloid origin of the Hyksos. M. Naville has very clearly shown that both these opinions are not incompatible with the history of the foreign invasion. He says : ' The presence of a Turanian race in Mesopotamia at a remote epoch is no more questioned by most Assyriologists. It does not mean that the whole bulk of the invaders, the entire population that settled in Egypt,

was of Turanian origin.   It would be contrary to well-established historical facts.   It is certain that all that remained in Egypt of the Hyksos, in the language, in the worship, in the name of *Aamu* by which they were called, everything points to a decidedly Semitic influence.   But the kings may very well not have been Semites.   How often do we see in Eastern monarchies and even in European states a difference of origin between the ruling class, to which the royal family belongs, and the mass of the people !   We need not leave Western Asia and Egypt ; we find there Turks ruling over nations to the race of which they do not belong, although they have adopted their religion.   In the same way as the Turks of Bagdad, who are Finns, now reign over Semites, Turanian kings may have led into Egypt and governed a population of mixed origin where the Semitic element was prevalent. If we consider the mixing up of races which took place in Mesopotamia in remote ages, the invasions which the country had to suffer, the repeated conflicts of which it was the theatre, there is nothing extraordinary that populations coming out of this land should have presented a variety of races and origins.   Therefore, I believe that though we cannot derive evidence from ethnological con-
· siderations, they do not oppose the opinion stated above that the starting point of the invasion of the Hyksos must be looked for in Mesopotamia, and that the conquest of Egypt by the shepherds was the consequence of the inroads of the Elamites into the valley of the Tigris and Euphrates.'

It must be clearly remembered that Manetho is the author of the name Hyksos as applied to these strangers. Nowhere on the Egyptian monuments does it occur. Probably the interpretation of the term is that it is a corruption of *hiq* or *haq*, meaning in the hieroglyphs a *prince* or *chieftain*, and *Shasu*, *nomads*, or *wanderers.*—ED.]

This brings us to the close of the Middle Empire. During the 1,361 years that it lasted, many events crossed the fortunes of the kingdom.

Ushered in with the Eleventh Dynasty, the Middle Empire at its commencement found the country hesitating and divided as if recovering from an invasion ; and at its close an invasion was only too imminent : yet the Lake Mœris, the hypogea of Beni-Ḥaṣan and of Siût, the colossi of Sân and of Abydos, the obelisks of Mataríyeh and Begig,[6] show that between these two troubled periods Egypt saw some days of real glory.

[6] In the Fayûm. This obelisk is a variation on the general type. Instead of being a square, it is a rectangular oblong, and instead of being surmounted as usual by a pyramidion, the top is rounded off, forming a ridge, in the centre of which is a groove, probably used for the insertion of some emblem. This monument, originally monolithic, was 43 feet high, two of its sides are 6 ft. 9 in. wide, the other two 4 ft. It is now broken in two. From the inscriptions upon it, we find that it was erected by Usertsen I., and is consequently contemporaneous with the obelisk of Mataríyeh.

CHAPTER IV

HEATHEN PERIOD—THE NEW EMPIRE— DYNASTIES XVIII.—XXXI.

HARDLY were the Shepherds expelled than with the Eighteenth Dynasty [1] Egypt arose more vigorous than ever : and a marvellous vitality is one of the distinguishing features of this remarkable period of history. In a few years the country had regained all that the five centuries of Hyksos rule had caused her to lose. From the Mediterranean to Gebel-Barkal both banks of the Nile became decorated with temples, new roads for commerce were opened up, and agriculture, industry, and art all sprang into fresh life. The political *rôle* of the country now became immense. She sent her viceroys into the Sûdan as governors-general, and northwards her garrisons were stationed in Mesopotamia and along the banks of the Tigris and Euphrates.

The first king of this illustrious dynasty was Amosis, and the rapid impulse which carried Egypt to the zenith of her fame may be dated from the reign of this prince. Not content with clearing the country of the Hyksos, he

[1] B.C. 1703.

conducted an army into Palestine ; and afterwards, turning southwards, forced his way into Nubia. At the same time he rebuilt the temples which had been thrown down, and showed his devotion to the gods by the erection of new sanctuaries : while the marvellous jewellery which he caused to be made for the decoration of his mother's mummy shows how completely the country must have recovered its resources. Among the treasures at the Gizeh Palace there is nothing which shows such artistic workmanship as the regalia of Queen Aah-hotep ; and, looking at the long gold chain, the open work pectoral, the diadem with two sphinxes and the poignard with raised ornaments of damascened gold, it is difficult to believe that these objects came from Theban workshops, which must yet have been feeling the strain of a long and harassing invasion.

To Amosis succeeded Amenophis I., the tendency of whose policy was to enlarge the frontiers of Egypt, both north and south ; for from the monuments it is clear that he went armed into both Syria and the Sûdan. Thothmes I. followed him, and once more Egypt turned her eyes to much-coveted Ethiopia, where, in spite of the dreaded cataracts, the king ventured an army which returned victorious from the campaign. In the north a yet more daring undertaking has made the name of Thothmes famous. Beyond Palestine and the land of Canaan, in the heart of the plains watered by the Tigris and Euphrates, dwelt a people called in the hieroglyphs the Rutennu. What was before said of the Cushites will equally hold good with regard to these new people. The Rutennu possessed neither unity of race nor a definite territory. They already owned important towns like Nineveh and Babylon, though several of their tribes were still wanderers on the debateable borderland of the confederation. Their country even had no very distinct name, and although Mesopotamia, Babylon, and Assyria all formed part of it, it seems usually to have gone by the name of this last kingdom. What can have been the inducement to Thothmes I. to cross the desert which separated Assyria from Egypt will never be known. This much is certain, that Assyria as well as the Sûdan felt the weight of the Egyptian yoke, and the victories of Thothmes were recorded on stelæ erected upon the banks of the Euphrates and the Upper Nile. The reign of Thothmes marks an advance in the path of progress : from the time of his accession, Egypt strained every nerve, and from being the conquered she became suddenly the conqueror.

Thothmes I. reigned twenty-one years ; and, dying, left the crown to his son, Thothmes II. In his days the Sûdan was finally subjugated, and on the rocks at Assûan may be read for the first time, 'Royal Governor of the South Country,' this title being given to those functionaries who represented the authority of the crown on the further side of the cataracts. From no other source does it appear that Thothmes II. was a warrior king. He was succeeded by his brother Thothmes III., then probably a child. At his accession Hatshepsu, his sister—who had played an important part in public affairs under the late king—constituted herself his guardian.[2]

But her regency was in reality usurpation, and during the seventeen years of her government she assumed every prerogative of royalty. Her reign was most brilliant ; there is no monarch in all the annals of Egyptian history who, already so great in war, and having so strong a political influence, has left besides so many proofs of a true artistic taste. Amongst the chief works due to the initiative of this queen are the two great obelisks at Karnak, one of which yet stands among the ruins of the temple. From the inscriptions on them, we gather that they were dedicated to her father's memory. On the base of the obelisk, still upright, are inscribed some details worth mentioning. For instance, it is there stated that the upper part of both were once capped with pyramidions of pure gold, which had been taken as booty from conquered foes ; also that the erection of one of these monuments from the time that it was quarried in the hill-side of Assûan took but seven months. From this statement it is possible to estimate what efforts were necessary in order to transport, and then place upright, a mass weighing nearly 366 tons, and standing ninety-seven feet six inches high. The temple of Dêr-el-Bahari is yet

[2] From an inscription on the temple of Karnak we find that Queen Hatshepsu was the daughter of Thothmes I. and his queen Aahmes Nefertari ; Thothmes II., her eldest half brother and husband, was the son of Maut Nefer, a lady of inferior rank, while Thothmes III. was the son of Ast, who was a *royal mother* but not a *royal wife.*

another example of Queen Hatshepsu's magnificence. On its walls the military exploits of the queen are told in full ; and bas-reliefs, sculptured with marvellous boldness and vigour, describe all the incidents of a campaign under-taken against the land of Punt—a region in the southern part of the Arabian peninsula.[3] The terrible mutilations to which this temple has been subjected prevent us from learning in what particular combats the Egyptian soldiers distinguished themselves, though from the walls of two of the chambers we know that victory remained with the queen. There may be seen the Egyptian general re-ceiving as a suppliant the enemy's chieftain, whose skin is of a deep brown colour, while his hair falls in long thin locks over his shoulders. He is unarmed. Behind him follow his wife and daughter, the repulsive features of both of whom are portrayed by the Egyptian artist with inimitable skill. Their flesh hangs loosely and their legs are swelled, while large excrescences in various parts of their bodies seem to betoken some terrible malady. Elsewhere the vanquished are seen embarking the spoil taken after the battle. Here are giraffes, monkeys, leopards, arms, ingots of copper, and rings of gold ; there may be seen whole trees, probably of some rare species, with their roots enclosed in great boxes, full of earth. The vessels are large and strongly built, and may be propelled either by sails or oars. A goodly crew covers the deck : and thanks to the extreme care with which

[3] Later researches show that the land of Punt in Queen Hat- shepsu's day was the modern coast of Somali.

the artist has shown the arrangement of the masts and sails, and even of the knots of the complicated ropes which unite the different parts of the vessel, we are able to form a clear idea of a ship belonging to the Egyptian fleet 4,000 years ago.

In another chamber of this same temple are some equally interesting scenes. With measured step the Egyptian regiments enter Thebes triumphantly. Every soldier carries a palm branch in his left hand, while in his right is a pike or axe. The trumpeters go first, sounding fanfares, while officers carry shoulder-high the standard bearing the name of the victorious regent.

Hatshepsu was indeed worthy to be the sister of the Thothmes, and in the series of those illustrious sovereigns who made the Eighteenth Dynasty famous, and left their footsteps so deeply imprinted upon Egyptian history, she holds no insignificant place. The accession of Thothmes III. constituted no reason why she should abdicate the attributes of royalty which for seventeen years she had arrogated to herself; and as in the reign of Thothmes II., so now did she take part in public affairs. At her death, he, whose power she had usurped, found himself completely master of the country. Of all the Pharaohs who in turn guided the destinies of the kingdom, none so truly deserves the title of Great as Thothmes III., in whose reign Egypt reached the zenith of her glory. At home a careful organization of the country's resources secured everywhere order and progress; and many

splendid edifices were raised at Wady-Magharah, Heliopolis,[4] Memphis, Thebes, Ombos,[5] Elephantiné, and in
Nubia.   Abroad Egypt became in consequence of her
victories mistress of the world.   She added yet again to
her conquests in the Sûdan, and there still exists a list
of several viceroys who in the name of Thothmes III.
exercised sovereign power over this distant province.
The Egyptian fleet at this time seized upon Cyprus ;
and, after eighteen years of perpetual fighting, all eastern
Asia was conquered.   Under this great king, Egypt, to
use the poetic expression of the time, '*placed her frontiers
where she would.*'   Her empire consisted of the whole of
Abyssinia, the Sûdan, Nubia, Egypt Proper, Syria, Mesopotamia, Irak-Arabia, Kurdistan, and Armenia.   Reckoning from the death of his brother, Thothmes III. reigned
forty-seven years, and at his death left the kingdom more
powerful, more influential, and more dreaded than it had
ever been before.

His son, Amenophis II., succeeded him, and in ten
years' time was followed by Thothmes IV., who reigned
thirty-one years.   The policy of both these princes was
to preserve what their great ancestor had conquered for
them, and to their praise be it said that they succeeded.

The accession of Amenophis III. was the signal for
fresh struggles.   The self-praise of the king may be read
to-day upon the architraves of the temple at Luxor, and
posterity allows that it is not exaggerated.   'He is the
Horus, the powerful bull ; he who rules by fire and sword

---

[4] On.   [5] Kom-Ombo.

and destroys the barbarians—the king of Upper and
Lower Egypt, absolute master, Son of the Sun. He
smites the heads over all countries, none can stand before
his face. He marches like the conquering Horus, the
son of Isis ; as the sun in the heavens ; he overthrows
fortresses. By his valour he causes all nations to pay
tribute to Egypt ; he—the lord of both worlds—the
Son of the Sun.' Amenophis III. was as great in peace
as in war. In his reign Egypt lost none of her military
prestige, and from some large scarabæi—one of which is
in the Gizeh Palace—we learn that under his rule Egypt
stretched from Mesopotamia to the country of Karo in
Abyssinia. At the same time that he consolidated the
empire left him by preceding monarchs, Amenophis
raised along the banks of the Nile monuments, which, for
their grandeur and the perfection of their workmanship,
are unsurpassed. The temple at Gebel-Barkal, in the
Sûdan, was erected by this king ; so also was that at
Soleb, near the Third Cataract—and souvenirs of him may
be found at Assûan, Elephantiné, Gebel-Silsileh, El-Kab,
Tûrah, the Serapēum at Memphis, and Serbût-el-Hadim.[6]
He added considerably to Karnak, and built that portion
of the temple at Luxor that bears his name. He also
erected on the left bank of the Nile—opposite to Luxor
—a sacred edifice which once must have been one of
the most important in Egypt. Destroyed completely by
causes unknown to us, all that is now left of it are the
two enormous colossi—called by the Arabs Sânamat—

[6] In the Sinaitic Peninsula.

which originally stood at the entrance.   Until the year
B.C. 27 these colossal portraits of the king attracted no
more attention than did any other statues ; but an earth-
quake in that year caused the greater part of one of them
to fall down.   It was then discovered that from the base,
still left in its original position, was emitted at sunrise a
prolonged sound caused by the warming of the dew that
had fallen during the night.   To the Greeks and Romans,
who then travelled a great deal in Egypt, this phenomenon
formed an immense attraction, and soon the statue of
Amenophis was transformed into the image of King
Memnon, who at sunrise saluted his divine mother—The
Dawn.   This poetic legend has been the cause of those
numberless Greek and Latin inscriptions that have been
engraved on the legs of the colossus.

Amenophis III. was succeeded by Amenophis IV.,
who followed the warlike example of his predecessors,
inasmuch as in the bas-reliefs of the Tell-el-Amarna
tombs the king, in his chariot, accompanied by his seven
daughters, is seen treading under foot the conquered
Asiatics.   But Nature did not endow this monarch with
wisdom equal to his valour.   He seems to have been the
victim of religious fanaticism, and was the first of the long
line of Egyptian kings who dared to bring about a reformation.   Amen, the supreme deity, was proscribed, and in
the place of this god, so long venerated at Thebes,
Amenophis substituted the worship of Aten (the solar
disc), who not unreasonably has been compared to the
Adonaï of the Semites.   The king even changed his own

name, which literally means 'Peace of Amen,' to that of Khu-en-Aten, i.e. 'The splendour of the Sun's disc.' The blow thus levelled at the ancient dogmas had most disastrous consequences for Egypt. The temples dedicated to Amen were spoiled, while the erection of Tell-el-Amarna as the new capital caused Thebes to lose much of its ancient glory. The hypogea of Tell-el-Amarna clearly show that Khu-en-Aten's mother (Thi), who all along had sympathized with her son's religious opinions, felt herself quite at home in the sudden change of tenets which took place in the country. That she was not an Egyptian is clearly shown in the representations of her at Thebes (Abû Hamed), where she is depicted with the fair skin of the Northern women. On a scarab in the Gizeh Palace she is described as the daughter of parents who were not only not of the blood royal, but must have been of foreign race, as their names even are not Egyptian.[7]   In raising altars to a god hitherto unknown to the Egyptians, Amenophis IV. was only reverting to his national type; he was doing the very same thing for Aten which the Hyksos had before done for

---

[7] Jua and Thua. We now know that Thi was a daughter of Tushratta, king of Mitanni—probably the Maten of the hieroglyphs, the Aram Naharaim of the Old Testament—that Amenophis III., while on a hunting expedition in that country, fell in love with her, and eventually made her his queen, and that he took her away to her new home, accompanied by 317 of her ladies. Doubtless it was from his Semitic mother that Khu-en-Aten learnt the worship of the solar disc.

Sutekh. At court the foreign element predominated ; at least that is the only explanation that can be given of the Tell-el-Amarna bas-reliefs, which depict the king with features absolutely non-Egyptian, surrounded by functionaries to whom the artist has given a physiognomy as curious as their master's.[8]

After several insignificant kings[9] came Horus (Hor-em-heb), and with him the series of legitimate princes begins again ; but with him there also set in a violent reaction against the fanatical reforms of Amenophis IV. The names of the dethroned kings were everywhere chiselled out : their buildings were razed to the ground, and the capital at Tell-el-Amarna was so carefully and patiently demolished that not one stone is left standing. Horus appears to have been a wise king, who knew how to maintain the superiority of Egypt, and to keep possession of those distant frontiers conquered by Thothmes III., which, according to the obelisk at Constantinople, stretched to the

[8] For some time past it had been an ascertained fact that the tombs of Khu-en-Aten and his family were known at any rate to the Arabs. In 1889 the jewellery of Queen Neferti-iti was bought in Luxor ; in the following year the funerary scarab of Khu-en-Aten, a beautiful bloodstone set in gold, was purchased, and this year I was fortunate enough to get his signet ring. It is of massive gold and bears the royal cartouche supported on a sacred boat. M. Grébaut has now announced the 'find' of the tomb of Khu-en-Aten, but of course it has been completely rifled, and is terribly knocked about, while the despoiled mummy was in all probability long ago destroyed.

[9] Amenophis IV.'s three sons-in-law and his master of the horse.

furthest borders of Mesopotamia. Horus was the last
Pharaoh of that Eighteenth Dynasty, which during the
241 years that it lasted brought so much glory to
Egypt.

With the Nineteenth Dynasty opens one of the most
brilliant periods of Egyptian history, but notwithstanding
the splendour which surrounds the story of some of these
great warrior kings, there are signs which betoken coming
trouble, and Egypt, formerly so menacing, was herself
soon to become perpetually menaced.

The first of this new series of kings was Ramses I.,
and of his reign there are but few monuments. It is
known that he conducted a campaign into that large tract
of country lying to the north of Syria and between the
left bank of the Euphrates, the Taurus Mountains, and
the sea. Here we again meet with the god Sutekh and
his worshippers, and here also dwelt the Khetas,[1] a most
powerful nation, who, like the neighbouring Rutennu,
appear to have been at the head of a whole confederation
of tribes. If an inscription at Karnak may be believed,
Ramses was the first king who went as far as the Orontes
to encounter the Khetas. No other military achievement
marked his reign. He was succeeded by Seti I., the
Sethos of Greek tradition. I have already said what
were the limits of the kingdom of Egypt in the time of
Thothmes III. ; but if the battles of Seti I., as depicted
upon the walls of Karnak, be studied, it will be found

[1] A Semitic people, and pos-   the descendants of Heth (Gen.
sibly identical with the Hittites,   xxiii. 3).

that this prince had to undertake the very same campaigns as had his illustrious ancestor before him. Again were the Shasu and the people of Punt made to submit, and again had Egyptian garrisons to be sent into Syria, and the Khetas and Rutennu reconquered. Nineveh and Babylon were also attacked, and even into Armenia did the king carry his victorious arms. So early as the second reign of the Nineteenth Dynasty, Western Asia, by repeated revolts, protested against the sovereignty of Egypt, and it is quite possible that, little as they were able to strengthen themselves against her, these people that had hitherto been treated as unsubmissive vassals, proved themselves not only formidable enemies, but well-nigh masters of the situation. The foreign wars to which Seti I. went do not appear to have prevented him from turning his attention to the arts of peace, and the internal prosperity of the country may be gauged by those magnificent buildings which are still the wonder and delight of travellers. There is the great hypostyle hall at Karnak, one of the masterpieces of Egyptian architecture, and the grand temple of Abydos with its incomparable bas-reliefs ; while the boldness of the architect who excavated the subterranean tomb of the king at Bab-el-Molûk [2] fills us with astonishment and admiration. Nor must it be forgotten that Seti was the first king who joined the Red Sea and the Nile by a canal, and who, by sinking an artesian well in the mountain, opened up

At Thebes.

the caravan road leading from Radasîeh to the gold mines of Gebel-Atoki.[3]

Ramses II., his successor, reigned sixty-seven years, and had 170 children, fifty-nine of whom were princes.[4] He was indeed the builder king *par excellence*, and, go where you will in Egypt, there is never a ruin nor an ancient Tell whereon his name may not be found. The two temples of Abû-Simbel, the Ramessēum at Thebes, the small temple at Abydos are all his, and at Memphis, in the Fayûm, and at Sân he erected many large buildings. It is partly owing to his long reign that Ramses II. was able to carry out so many important works; and also due to his wars which provided him with an immense number of prisoners who, according to Egyptian custom, were employed in the erection of public edifices. These causes may also account for the presence of numerous foreign tribes whom the fertility of the soil, and the policy of the Government, drew from the Asiatic plains to the Nile side, and who in return for the hospitality which Egypt gave them furnished workmen for the cutting of canals and the building of temples and towns. It was for this same Ramses that the Israelites in the Eastern Delta built the town bearing his name.[5]

The wars of Ramses II. show that the anxiety betrayed at the commencement of the Nineteenth

[3] Here also was built a small temple 'to the name of King Seti,' the ruins of which are still visible.

[4] The Temple of Abydos gives 119 children; 60 sons and 59 daughters.

[5] See Egypt Exploration Fund Memoirs, No. IV.

Dynasty was not without foundation, and the time was now not far off when Egypt would cease to be the arbiter of the world's destinies. The reaction necessary for this was just beginning. In the north, south, and west, the peoples conquered by the Thothmes and Amenophises were beginning to revolt against their old masters. The Sûdan waxed restless, and the temple walls are covered with representations of the victories gained by the princes of Ethiopia over their turbulent vassals. At the same time the northern provinces were threatened by, and with difficulty defended from, an incursion of fair-haired, blue-eyed nomads who, coming originally from the islands in the Mediterranean, took possession of the desert on the western side of the delta.

In Asia the same reactionary spirit against Egypt was abroad. There, joining with twenty other tribes, the chariot-fighting Khetas formed an alliance against Ramses; and after a struggle which lasted eighteen years, the king was only so far successful as to conclude a treaty of peace, at once as favourable to them as to himself, with the very people whom not long before he had spoken of as 'the vile race of the Khetas.' It was during this long campaign that Ramses II. displayed before his whole army so great a proof of personal courage that it became the subject of the great historical poem of Pentaur, which was engraven on the northern face of the pylon of the temple at Luxor, and on one of the outside walls of Karnak. It was in the fifth year of his reign, on the ninth day of the month Epiphi, that Ramses was advancing with his army

upon the town of Kadesh. Deceived by the Bedâwin
scouts employed by the Kheta king, Ramses fell into
an ambuscade, and was immediately surrounded by the
enemy's troops. The Egyptians, taken by surprise,
immediately fled, and Ramses found himself alone.
'Then,' says the poet, singing his master's praises, 'the
king—life, health, and strength be to him—arose like
his father, Mentu,[6] and grasped his weapons . . . and
rushed in his chariot into the midst of the army of the
vile Khetas. He was quite alone : no one was with him.
He found himself surrounded by 2,500 chariots, and beset
by the bravest heroes of the miserable Khetas and their
allies—from Arathu, Masu, Pidasa, Kishkish, Malunna,
Quazauadana, Khilibu, Akirith, Kadesh, and Leka.
Each chariot had three men, but the king had neither
his princes, nor generals, nor captains of archers, nor
chariots with him.' In this perilous condition Ramses
called upon the supreme deity of Egypt :—

'My archers and horsemen have forsaken me, there
is no one left to fight with me. What does my Father
Amen mean? Is he a father that will forsake his son?
. . . Have I not done according to thy command-
ments, O my Father? Did not thy mouth guide my
expeditions, and thy counsels have they not directed me?
Have I not made many great feasts in thine honour, and
filled thy temples with the spoils of war? The whole
world has consecrated its offerings to thee ; I have sacri-
ficed 30,000 bullocks to thee with sweet-smelling herbs

[6] The Egyptian war god.

and perfumes. I have builded thee temples of stone, and
raised masts[7] in thine honour for all time. For thee I
have brought obelisks from Elephantiné and everlasting
stones. I caused ships to go for thee across the sea to
bring to thee the tribute of all nations. . . . From the
midst of unknown peoples I call to thee, O my .
Father. I am alone—none is with me to help : my
archers and charioteers have deserted me; when I called
they would not hear. But Amen is more to me than
thousands of archers, thousands of charioteers, and
myriads of young heroes all united together.'

After this touching lament the poet puts this reply
into the mouth of the god : ' Thy words have found an
echo in Hermonthis,[8] O Ramses. I, thy father, am near
to thee. My hand is with thee, and I am more to thee
than millions of men. . . . By my aid shall the 2,500
chariots be dashed in pieces before thy horses. The
hearts of thine enemies shall fail, and their limbs faint ;
they shall neither hurl their arrows nor find courage to
thrust with the spear. I will cause them to throw themselves into the waters as do the crocodiles, they shall fall
one upon another and shall slay one another. Not one
shall look behind him, and every one that falls shall
never rise up again.' During this time the charioteer of
Ramses, standing by his master's side, sees the enemy's
hosts closing round them, and he addresses the king thus :

---

[7] An allusion to the festival
masts placed in front of the
pylons of an Egyptian temple.

[8] In the neighbourhood of
Thebes, and dedicated to Mentu·

'Oh, my good lord, brave king, the sole protector of
Egypt in the day of combat ; we are alone in the midst
of the foe ; stay and let us save the breath of our lives.
What can we do, my good lord Ramses ? '

The king replied : ' Courage, O my charioteer, and
.strengthen thine heart. I will dash into the midst of
them like the divine hawk⁹ himself. I will overthrow
them, and slay them, and they shall bite the dust.' . . .
Ramses then charged the enemy six times, and each time
struck down their chief warriors. After this he called
together his own generals and horsemen, who had taken
no part in the combat, and said : ' You are of no good
to me nor to the country. If I, your master, had not
stood firm, you would have all perished. You stayed in
your dwellings and in your fortresses, and were of no help
to the army. I sent word to each in his own place to
watch for the day and the hour of the battle, and you
have all acted badly. A worse deed than I can tell has
been done by my soldiers and my horsemen. I have
shown my valour alone, for neither archers nor horsemen
were with me. The whole world is witness of the strength
of my arm ; I was alone : no one was with me.'

After these words the poem carries us on to the
evening when the army of Ramses arrived. ' They found
all the region through which they marched covered with
corpses bathed in blood; there was hardly place to stand,
so numerous were the bodies.' Then the generals ad-
dress the king : ' Great warrior of dauntless courage, thou

⁹ Mentu.

hast been the saviour of thine archers and horsemen. Very son of Tmu, thou hast by thine own sword annihilated the Khetas.   There is no other king like unto thee, thou lord of victory, who fights for his soldiers in the day of battle.   Thou, O brave one, art first in the fight. Thou art the bravest of the brave, before thine own army, and in the face of the whole world.'   To which Ramses replies : ' Not one of you has done well thus to leave me alone in the midst of mine enemies.   Neither princes nor captains strengthened my hands.   I fought alone, and withstood thousands of peoples.   My horses " Victory in Thebes," and " Maut is satisfied," they it was who helped me when I was all alone in the midst of foes. Henceforth each day when I am in my palace their corn shall be given them before the god Phra.'

The next day at dawn Ramses prepared again for battle, and hurled himself into the fray like a bull among geese.   ' His warriors likewise dashed into the fight like as a hawk swoops down upon its prey.   The great lion who accompanied the king's horses fought for him, he was full of fury, and every one who came in his way was overthrown.   The king fell upon them and killed them ; not one of them escaped.   Trampled to pieces by his horses, their bodies lay stretched out and bathed in gore.' A few more lines close this narrative.[1]

The Khetas were completely routed, and a peace

---

[1] The passages here quoted are from M. de Rougé's edition. Professor E. L. Lushington has published an English translation in ' Records of the Past,' vol. ii. p. 65 *et seq.*

signed by both sovereigns put an end provisionally to the war. That Ramses was a great warrior the above details will have shown, while from Gebel-Barkal to Nahr-el-Kelb, near Beyrût, there are inscriptions attesting the exploits of him whom the Greeks praised by the name of Sesostris. Impartial history, aided by the monuments, shows the conquests of Ramses II. to have been exaggerated, and it is possible that writers of ancient classic tradition may have attributed to him alone all those feats of arms which made the names of Thothmes III., Seti I., and Ramses III., celebrated. His thirteenth son and successor was Merenptah, in whose reign the Israelites under Moses fled from Egypt : he was, therefore, that Pharaoh who perished in the Red Sea.[2] His tomb may still be seen in the valley of Bab-el-Molûk. After three other reigns in which nothing worthy of notice occurred, the Nineteenth Dynasty died out, having lasted 174 years.

The Twentieth Dynasty was ushered in brilliantly by Ramses III., who proved himself a worthy successor to his illustrious ancestors. Medinet Habû, at Thebes, is

[2] There is only one verse in the Bible which implies even that Pharaoh was drowned, Ps. cxxxvi. 15, in which it is said that 'God shook off Pharaoh and his host into the Red Sea.' In every other place the writer carefully evades a definite statement : Exodus xiv. 23–25, 28 ; xv. 4, 19, 21, &c. A papyrus in the Berlin Museum states that Merenptah lost a son by a very sudden death. He appears to have been a great coward, and very cruel. Lenormant says of him : 'He was neither a soldier nor an administrator, but a man whose whole mind turned upon sorcery and magic.' The probability is that Merenptah himself did not take the field on this occasion.

E

the pantheon dedicated to the glory of this new Pharaoh.
Every pylon, every door, every chamber in it tells of his
exploits. Once again the land of Punt is subjugated,
and forced to pay tribute ; Cush receives just punishment
for its many revolts ; the Libyans, who again re-appear
upon the western frontiers, are severely defeated ; and in
the north, war is resumed this time on sea as well as land.
The Khetas, who were conquered by Ramses II., rise
against Ramses III., and are aided by the Zakkar[3] and
the Philistines from the coasts of Syria ; while the Cy-
priotes furnished a contingent to help the confederate
armies. Close to an unknown town near the sea shore
the hostile fleets met. A hand-to-hand fight ensued, and
the bas-reliefs at Medinet Habû represent the Egyptians'
foes being thrown head first into the waves which
swallowed them. While this took place Ramses III.
remained on shore to repulse the attacks of the allied
armies. Like Ramses II., he had a tame lion close to
his chariot, who fought for him and devoured the fallen
enemies. The Twentieth Dynasty opened brightly, and
under it the ancient glory of Egypt seemed to revive ;
but the timid successors of the hero of Medinet Habû
did not know how to keep intact the treasures bequeathed
to them, and the brilliant victories of Ramses III. were
in vain to arrest Egypt from the downfall she was so soon
to experience.

Although she sent her governors into Syria, their

[3] Sayce identifies the Zak-   east coast of Cyprus.
kar with the Teucrians on the

authority was but fictitious ; and the country by her prolonged contact with the Asiatics was losing that unity
wherein lay her strength. She allowed Semitic words to
creep into the national tongue, and foreign deities invaded
her hitherto inaccessible sanctuaries. At Thebes the
high priests of Amen, profiting by the inertness of the
last kings of the Twentieth Dynasty, gradually undermined
the royal power, and even aspired to the dethronement
of the lawful monarchs. Thus had Egypt to pay for the
ambition of the conquering kings of the Eighteenth
Dynasty. Humiliated where before she had been so
powerful, she was yet destined to see the land trodden
under the feet of strangers, and, after having conquered
the Cushites, the Libyans, and the Asiatics, was at last
forced to receive her kings from them. It was because
she was not content to remain upon territory which was
really her own, i.e. the banks of the Nile as far as they
stretched to the south, and because she forced herself,
where the conditions both of race and climate compro-
mised her authority, that the kingdom, already too large,
fell to pieces. It is the close of the finest period
in Egyptian history. Powerless in the face of so
many dangers, the empire of Mena, after the reign of
Ramses III., moves sadly towards its ruin. One by one,
both in north and south, Egypt's conquests slipped from
her grasp, and at the time when, under the last monarch
of the Twentieth Dynasty, the high priests forcibly
appropriated the crown of the Pharaohs, she was
reduced to her smallest limits and surrounded by

enemies from henceforth more powerful than herself.

During the Twenty-first Dynasty the empire was literally torn in two. At Thebes reigned the self-made kings of the sacerdotal caste : while at Tanis arose the dynasty admitted by Manetho to be legitimate. From this moment Egypt lost her hold over Asia, and indications are not wanting to show that already Asiatic influence was increasing along the Nile. The Theban kings chose Semitic names for their sons ; while the princes of Sân sent an Egyptian princess to the harem of Solomon.[4]

The Twenty-second Dynasty (B.C. 980) chose Bubastis or its capital. It does not appear to have given many conquerors to Egypt. Its first king, the Shishak of the Bible, the Shashanq of the monuments, took an army into Palestine and carried away the treasures of the Temple.[5] It is surprising to find how many members of this royal family bear Assyrian names, such as Nimrod, Tiglath, or Sargon ; also that the regiment whose special duty it was to guard the king's person was composed not of Egyptians but of the Mashuasha, a Libyan tribe, whom Ramses III. had so often routed from the frontiers of the Delta. This intelligence, gained from the discovery of monuments during the excavations at the Serapēum, is the key to the history of this and the following dynasties. Befor this Egypt's tendency was to expand, now her chief

[4] I Kings iii. 1 ; vii. 8 ;   [5] Kings xiv. 25-26.
ix. 16-24 ; xi. 1.

object was to concentrate herself; and where aforetime
she had imposed her laws upon the neighbouring
nations, she now had to submit to those of foreigners.
Never again was there to arise a Memphite or a Theban
dynasty ; and Egypt, fascinated by Asia, had her capitals
from henceforth in the Delta. From the time of the
Twenty-second Dynasty, Egypt was never again her own
mistress. Under the Theban families she could with
impunity open her doors and give a portion of her
territory to certain foreign tribes—as she did to the
Israelites—knowing that by her prestige alone she could
control them. But now all was changing. These very
tribes not only rose up against her, but even aspired to
become lords of that soil which was theirs by courtesy only.

Once more was Egypt compelled to bow to Destiny,
and the coming in of the Twenty-second Dynasty was
but the accession to the throne of one of those foreign
families from the eastern frontiers of the Delta.

Most unlooked-for events ushered in the Twenty-
third Dynasty. From causes as yet unknown to us,
Egypt was completely divided within herself. In the
north, instead of becoming a separate kingdom, as in the
days of the Hyksos, we find her split up into several little
states, and domineered over by a handful of petty kings
—veritable janissaries—drawn for the most part from the
ranks of the Mashuasha, who probably by slow degrees
scaled the steps of the throne. In the south a state of
affairs still more unforeseen betrayed the internal discords
which prevailed in the unhappy country. The Sûdan,

which until now had been submissive to the Pharaohs, suddenly arose as an organised and independent kingdom. No longer were 'Governors of the South' and 'Princes of Cush' to carry out above the Cataract the orders issued from Thebes or Memphis; the land of Cush was free, and Upper Egypt as far as Minieh was but a province of the Sûdan.

According to Manetho, the Twenty-fourth Dynasty consisted of one solitary king called Bocchoris, who reigned six years.[6]   Whether he expelled the Cushites from Upper Egypt, or whether he was but one of those partial kings of the north who united Lower Egypt under one sceptre, has not yet been discovered.   It is certain that, soon after the accession of Bocchoris, Sabaco swooped through the Cataracts, fell upon the unfortunate king, burnt him alive, and took possession of his country as far as the Mediterranean.   How far away in the past do those great battles of Thothmes III. seem, when, as the conquering Pharaoh, he imposed tribute upon the '*vile race of Cush !*'   Now it is Cush who treats Egypt as a vanquished country, and reigns in the palaces that were once full of the glories of the Amenophises and Ramses.   With the Ethiopian rule, which lasted fifty years, the Twenty-fifth Dynasty closes, and this brings the history of Egypt to about B.C. 665.

The last king of this dynasty was Taharaqa ; he had

---

[6] Mariette recognises this king as the same as Uah-ka-Bak-en-ran-ef, whose Apis Sarophagus, together with that of the deceased Apis of the 37th year of Shashanq IV.'s reign, was deposited in one chamber of the Serapēum.

been reigning twenty-six years when twelve Egyptian
chiefs joined together, expelled the Ethiopians from the
northern provinces, and divided all the country they
were successful in reclaiming into twelve portions, over
which they made themselves kings. It is a curious fact
that, at the end of the Ethiopian domination, Egypt was
exactly in the same position as she had been when she
submitted for the first time to the yoke of the Sûdan.
In the north was this dodecarchy composed of allied
Egyptians, or perhaps even of Mashuasha ; in the south,
Thebes, under Piankhi and his queen Ameniritis, was for
the second time reduced to the condition of a province
of the Sûdan. Tired of foreign rule, Egypt retraced her
steps, and when Psammetichus came to the throne, she
seemed to have resumed history at the end of the Twenty-
second Dynasty.

The rule of the twelve kings lasted but fifteen years.
An oracle had foretold that Egypt should belong to
him who should drink water from a brazen cup. One
day, as the twelve princes were about to pour out their
libations, the high priest found—when presenting to them
the golden cups which they were accustomed to use—
that he had mistaken the number, and brought but
eleven.

Psammetichus, seeing that he had no cup like the
others, took off his brass helmet, and used it as a libation
vessel. The kings at once understood the purport of this
act, and a speedy exile into the marshes of the Delta was
the consequence. But Psammetichus was determined

to avenge himself for this outrage, so in his turn he sent
to consult an oracle, which told him that he should
be avenged by brazen men coming out of the sea.
At first he could not persuade himself that brazen men
could come to his help ; but shortly afterwards some
Greeks who were shipwrecked off the coast landed fully
armed. An Egyptian hastened to the marshes to take
the news to Psammetichus ; but as the messenger had
never before seen men armed in this manner, he said
that brazen men from the sea were pillaging the country.
The king then knew that the oracle had spoken truly,
made an alliance with the Greeks, and by many promises
won them over to take his part. Then, with his auxi-
liaries, and those Egyptians who remained faithful to
him, he set out on a campaign, dethroned the eleven
kings, overturned the Ethiopians, and won back for
Egypt her old territory from the Mediterranean to the
First Cataract. This new dynasty, of which Psammetichus
was the first king, corresponds to the Twenty-sixth of
Manetho : and the ruins close to the modern village of
Sâ-el-Hâgar[7] mark the site chosen for the official residence of its kings. There are many little indications
that favour the opinion that Psammetichus was not an
Egyptian, and that history is not so far wrong in think-
ing him a descendant of one of those Mashuasha imported
into the *corps d'élite* of the Egyptian army.[8] The Twenty-
sixth Dynasty, therefore, ought to be called Libyan.

[7] Saïs.
[8] Psammetichus was the son of Necho I., and grandson of the petty king Tefnekht.

Notwithstanding its extraction, and that its kings were not always fortunate in their foreign enterprises, Egypt enjoyed 138 years of prosperity. Psammetichus attempted the conquest of Asia, but only succeeded in besieging a town for twenty-nine years.[9] Necho II., one of his descendants,[1] tried in his turn to revive Egypt's old pretensions to the plains watered by the Tigris and Euphrates ; but he was defeated by Nebuchadnezzar at Carchemish, and found his only safety in flight.   Finally, Apries, another king, was disastrously beaten in Cyrenia, whither he had despatched an army.   Under the Saïte kings, Egypt's fame in war, which once was world-wide, nearly perished : though they endeavoured to redeem the unsuccessfulness of their campaigns by the care they took in restoring and rebuilding the old sanctuaries.   At Saïs were erected those wonderful porticoes which Herodotus placed above all others that he had seen in Egypt ; and which, like this celebrated town itself, have entirely disappeared.   To show the impulse given to civilization by the successors of Psammetichus, we need only mention their efforts to open up commerce and industry in new regions of Arabia, Greece, Syria, and along the eastern coast of the Mediterranean.   Although Necho's attempt to reopen the canal of Seti I., between the Red Sea and the Nile, was a failure, history must always give him his due for an enterprise which for those days was most daring, viz., the sending of a fleet from the Red Sea

[9] The Ashdod of the Old Testament ; the Azotus of the New Testament.   [1] His son.

across an ocean then unknown to the whole world, which rounded the Cape of Good Hope, and returned to Egypt by way of the western coast of Africa and the Straits of Gibraltar. The general policy of the Pharaohs of the Twenty-sixth Dynasty seems to have been to give all foreigners, but especially the Greeks, access to the country, and to admit young Greeks into the national schools, in order that they might learn Egyptian ; [2] in a word, to permit the great stream of liberal ideas then emanating from Greece to spread over the country, and so to revive the old monarchy founded by Mena. But, without knowing it, they were introducing a fresh element of decadence. Endowed as Egypt had been with both stability and a strong conservatism, she could not but lose by being brought into contact with this new element of civilization called Progress. The Greeks had hardly set foot in Egypt when it became easy to see that they would never leave it; and that with these two great principles brought face to face, one *must*, sooner or later, efface or absorb the other.

But a sudden catastrophe postponed the day when Greece should, in her turn, rule over Egypt. From those much-hankered-after Mesopotamian plains was marching in hot haste a semi-barbarous people who, having taken Susa and Babylon, and forced Syria to pay it tribute, was, within six months of the accession of Psammetichus III., at the very doors of Egypt. Over the hosts that the

---

[2] Hence arose the class of interpreters of which the modern   survivors are the dragomans.

Persians had brought with them, Cambyses, the son of Cyrus, was commander-in-chief. It was in vain that Psammetichus went to Pelusium to confront the enemy sent against his country ; his efforts were futile, and soon Egypt, snatched from her rightful owners, became only a province of the Persian Empire.[3] The first years of Cambyses' reign were peaceful. According to a statue in the Vatican, the hieroglyphs upon which have been translated by M. de Rougé, this king adored the Egyptian gods, and received instruction in those sciences for which the Egyptian priests were so celebrated. Thus passed five years, after which time a series of reverses followed his hitherto victorious arms. First of all, an expedition was sent against the Carthaginians, which was put to flight. Then a campaign into the Oasis of Ammon—in the western desert—was organised, but being betrayed by treacherous guides, and badly provisioned, the soldiers of Cambyses strayed into the desert, and not one ever returned to tell by what catastrophe a whole army had perished. At last, at the head of a very large body of troops, Cambyses himself started for the Sûdan ; but in this case, again, want of foresight was the ruin of the force, and after being only a few days in the desert between Egypt and the Sûdan, the soldiers became destitute and were obliged to retreat. Cambyses, after this third disaster, became furious. From Assûan to Thebes, from Thebes to Memphis, his route was marked by one continuous line of ruins. The temples were destroyed, and

[3] B.C. 527.

even the tombs of the kings were broken open and pillaged. The day of his arrival in Memphis was a great feast-day, and, hearing the sounds of rejoicing, his anger knew no bounds, for he believed that the Egyptians were holding high festival over his defeat. This was the beginning of a troublous time for Egypt ; but fortunately Cambyses soon died, an event which, although it put a stop to the devastations ordered by this mad conqueror, by no means brought the Persian rule to an end. Vainly Darius tried by his wise administration to make the people forget the yoke which weighed so heavily upon them ; the number-less ruins left by Cambyses spoke too loudly for that, and perpetual revolts showed that the country was deter-mined to avenge herself for injuries which she could not forget. Apparent submissions, followed by fresh insur-rections, lasted for 121 years, when good fortune gave Egypt back to her own people, and the Persians were forced to fly. The Twenty-seventh Dynasty then came to an end.

The sixty-seven years that followed (Dynasties XXVIII.—XXX.) were spent by the nation in repairing the disasters brought upon them by the late foreign occupation ; while Persia only waited for an opportunity to again seize upon the country she had so regretfully given up. Both nations made formidable preparations for a deadly encounter. But fate again betrayed the Egyptian arms, and although in the first battle Nectanebo I. chased the Persian general across the frontier, yet at Pelusium, Bubastis, and Memphis

Nectanebo II. was obliged to submit to superior force. He fled into the Sûdan, and for the second time the Persians became masters of Egypt. With him disappeared for ever the old race of Pharaohs.

History has little to say about the second Persian Dynasty. It had hardly been in power for eight years when, in the days of Darius III., Alexander appeared, and what could Egypt—already half conquered—do against the Macedonian hero? Tired out by the ever-increasing weight of the Persian yoke, she opened her gates to him as to a liberator, and thus after having been Ethiopian under the Twenty-fifth Dynasty, Libyan under the Twenty-sixth, and Persian under the Twenty-seventh and Thirty-first Dynasties, Egypt became Greek under the new master that the fortunes of war gave her.

So passed away the New Empire after an existence of 1,371 years.

CHAPTER V

THE short reign of Alexander the Great opens the
Thirty-second Dynasty ;[1] but, short as it was, it gave him
time to lay the foundations of the city, which ever since
has preserved his name; above all, it enabled him to
inaugurate that liberal-minded and tolerant policy which
gave to Egypt 275 years of peace and tranquillity in
theplace of trouble and disaster. From the day that
Alexander conquered the country he left the people
entire possession of their religion, manners and customs,
arts, language, and writing. We know from history that
he died in the midst of his victories; that his posthumous
son, Alexander II., succeeded him, and that until this
young prince's majority Egypt was governed by Philip
Arrhidœus, the conqueror's brother, as regent. We
know too that these ephemeral royalties did not prevent
Alexander's generals from dividing his empire between
them ; Egypt falling to the share of Ptolemy. With
him, therefore, arose a new dynasty, which was called

[1] B.C. 332.

from its founder the Ptolemaic.[2] To follow the details of these kings' reigns would be impossible : each called himself Ptolemy after his common ancestor, and among their wives we only find successions of Cleopatras, Berenices, and Arsinoës; while the history of the country is not of the same interest as when Egypt marched at the head of the nations. It mattered not whether they fought in the north or south, but the Pharaohs always fought for a civilization of which they were in a sense the incarnation : under the Ptolemies Egypt came down from her proud position ; she was no longer first among the nations, and no longer did she guide the world as in the days of Thothmes. She did indeed deteriorate, and from this time her history does but drag behind that of Greece. All the political actions of this period can be summed up in competitions for the throne, the rivalries of women, and inglorious struggles for Syria and the eastern islands of the Mediterranean. Yet, for all that, the Ptolemies deserve well of Egypt, and their names hold an honourable place among those monarchs who successively ruled over the country. No doubt this popularity was owing to their extreme tolerance. Far from imposing their foreign ways upon the conquered people, which would only have stirred up revolt, they maintained the ancient Egyptian customs, and without ceasing to be Greeks they became Egyptians, and prided themselves upon their adopted nationality. The temple of Edfû, which was built entirely by them,

[2] Dynasty XXXIII.

is a magnificent proof of their wise moderation. It was a Ptolemy who, after a fruitless campaign to the Tigris, returned to Egypt, bringing with him over 25,000 statues which had been carried away by Cambyses. A second and no less powerful cause also contributed to the reputation of the Ptolemies. Their names were coupled with the great intellectual movement which had its spring at Alexandria, and long exercised so decisive an influence upon the destinies of Egypt. It was, as we know, one of them who commanded Manetho to write the history of his country in Greek, and by whose orders the Greek translation of the Hebrew Scriptures known as the Septuagint was made.[3] Other and more important works keep their memories alive. That magnificent library at Alexandria, which it is said contained in 400,000 volumes all the Roman, Greek, Egyptian, and Indian literature, was founded by a Ptolemy, as well as the museum which has been justly regarded as the finest academy in the world.[4] Thus the Ptolemies, in making their capital the rendezvous of all the grammarians, savants, philosophers, and enlightened intellects of their time, laid the foundations of that great Alexandrian School of Philosophy which some centuries later contended with the infant Christianity for the supremacy of the world. Modest as was their *rôle* in politics and in war, these princes were justly celebrated for that love of letters and science which has been truly described as the genius of their race.

Ptolemy Alexander, dying without children, disposed

---

[3] Ptolemy Philadelphus.   [4] Ptolemy Soter.

of the kingdom of Egypt as if it had been a farm, and left the country of the Ramses by will to the Roman people ! The devices of the beautiful but crafty Cleopatra staved off for a few years the execution of the fatal contract. It was in vain that Cæsar and Mark Anthony tried to revive the dynasty of the Ptolemies. At Cleopatra's death the will of Ptolemy Alexander came into full effect, and in the year B.C. 30 Egypt was not only no longer a kingdom, but merely a province of that great empire of which Rome was the capital.

F

CHAPTER VI

HEATHEN PERIOD—ROMAN EPOCH—
DYNÀSTY XXXIV

ONCE mistress of the Nile, Rome did all that lay in her power to keep this her most valuable conquest. She left the religion, art, writing, language, and customs of Egypt unmolested, restored some ·of the temples, and built others, dedicating them to the gods of the country. Edfû, Esneh, Denderah, Erment, all begun by the Ptolemies, were completed under the Emperors. At Shêkh-Abâdeh [1] Hadrian built a town, and raised magnificent monuments to his favourite Antinoüs. Chapels were erected at Kalabsheh, Dabod, and Dendûr,[2] while new edifices at Philæ added to the grace and beauty of this lovely island. Having by these means made sure of removing from the conquered people their usual pretexts for discontent, Rome now decreed that the Egyptian towns should be garrisoned by her legions. At the head of the general administration of the country was placed a Roman official called the 'Augustan Prefect' of Egypt, who combined all offices in his own person, and governed uncontrolled

[1] In the province of Minieh.   [2] All in Nubia.

in the name of the Emperor. Rome, while quietly sub-
stituting herself for the legitimate masters of the country,
thus armed herself powerfully against revolts. It is true
that she reserved to herself the right of calling these all-
powerful prefects to account : their administration was
never a long one, and for the smallest shortcomings they
were punished with banishment or death ; moreover, it
was required by a law of the empire that the Prefects
of Egypt should not be chosen from among either the
senators or the patricians of rank. These measures did
not so much show that Rome regarded the conquered
and humiliated country with indifference, as that she
feared that the prestige of such a grand old kingdom
might tempt the ambition of one of these imperial
delegates whom force of circumstances had placed in a
position of such power.

Although the country itself enjoyed peace and prosperity under the wise and economical administration of
the Emperors, its own political life was dead. The credit
of the few warlike expeditions which were undertaken
must be given not to the Egyptians, who were probably
utterly indifferent to them, but to the Roman legions,
who alone took part in them. Petronius the Prefect
took an army into Arabia, and then turned south to
Gebel-Barkal, the capital of Ethiopia, to punish the
Queen Candace, who had dared to occupy Assûan and
ravage the Thebaïd. It is possible that these partial
revolts may have reminded them that Egypt had not
quite forgotten the glory of past days. Now it is a Syrian

of Alexandria who raises an army upon the proceeds of his only papyrus manufactory, and stirs up revolt against Rome. Then a certain Achilles, taking advantage of his power as Prefect of Egypt, caused himself to be proclaimed Emperor, and forced Diocletian to put Alexandria to fire and sword after besieging the town for eight months. But in these uprisings Egypt herself took no part; so long as the insurgents to whom she gave shelter succeeded in their efforts, she would have given Rome itself over to new masters without making any effort for her own independence. In two ways only did she manifest any vitality. Who does not remember that when Christianity was first brought into Egypt by St. Mark, terrible persecutions were endured by the believers in the new faith, and how much energy was displayed on the one hand to spread the new religion, and on the other hand to hinder it? Who also does not know the part played by the Alexandrian schools under Roman administration? Truly it may be said that Egypt at that moment reigned intellectually over both Greece and Rome, and extended her influence afar by the power of her thought. Yet, notwithstanding these rays of brilliant light, we feel that Egypt's part is played out, and her downfall complete. Thebes, Abydos, Memphis, Heliopolis, were in ruins; Alexandria was nothing but the chief town of a province, and Egypt, owing to the care bestowed upon her agriculture, sought for no higher glory than to be called 'the Granary of Rome.'

However, an event was at hand which not only influenced the future of the world, but gave a sudden turn to the destinies of Egypt. The Roman Empire, already too vast, was in its turn dismembered. In A.D. 364, two emperors divided it between them ; the one establishing his throne at Constantinople, the other remaining in Rome. In this division, Egypt, inclining towards the East, owned for her master the sovereign who reigned at the Bosphorus. This was the end. It was now some time since Christianity had first thrown out roots, and had little by little gained ground : now it was gradually working its way towards Constantinople. Egypt had already to a great extent accepted the new faith, though it was not yet officially acknowledged.

In A.D. 381, Theodosius, then reigning at Constantinople, promulgated the famous edict by which Christianity was to be henceforth the religion of Egypt. He also ordered that all the temples should be closed, and that the gods still venerated by the piety of the Egyptians should be destroyed. The annihilation of Heathen Egypt was now complete. Forty thousand statues are said to have perished, temples were profaned, mutilated, and destroyed ; and of its magnificent civilization, all that is now left are its ruins—more or less overthrown— and the monuments whose remains are to-day gathered together and given a home in our museums.

So closed—only two and a half centuries before the coming of Mahomet—the empire that 5,400 years before had been founded by Mena. We may indeed marvel at its enormous duration ; but Egypt owed this more to the condition of the world over which she exercised so remarkable an influence than to her own natural force. Her organisation, like that of China, was only adapted for immobility, not for progress. So long as the events of history brought across her path only those nations that, like herself, were stationary, she was admirably fitted to continue. But from the moment when Greece and Rome brought in the law of progress, she gradually became more and more feeble, and finally disappeared. Nations, like men, cannot live upon bread alone ; and the same law of Nature holds good for them as for us, that, failing progress, degeneration must ensue.

CHAPTER VII

THE CHRISTIAN PERIOD

WHEN the inhabitants of the Nile Valley gave up the religion of their forefathers and accepted Christianity, history no longer calls them Egyptians but Copts. The Copts, then, are the Christian descendants of that old race whose history we have been tracing. The period during which Christianity was the established religion of the country was but of short duration : it embraced the 259 years between the Edict of Theodosius, A.D. 381, and the conquest of Egypt by the lieutenants of Mahomet in A.D. 640. During this time, as has been already shown, Egypt followed the fortunes of the Roman Empire, and, the Empire becoming broken up, Egypt was attached to that part whose capital was at Constantinople, and for the 259 years prior to the Mussulman invasion was ruled by the Emperors of Byzantium. Although the religion of the Pharaohs had been abandoned, and Christianity adopted, the country still clung to the old language that had been spoken for so many centuries ; but the hieroglyphs whose symbols recalled heathen ideas were set aside, and the alphabet-writing of the Greeks as then used at Alexandria adopted. The Coptic language of to-day is therefore more or less the ancient Egyptian language applied to Christian use, and written with letters borrowed from a foreign script.

At the same time it must not be supposed that the year that issued the Edict of Theodosius saw the ancient national religion suddenly abandoned. The Edict certainly made Christian usages obligatory, but before the time of Theodosius there were already many Egyptians who had accepted Christianity ; as after it were found— especially in Upper Egypt—many who had difficulties in submitting to the new faith. It is not our intention to give here a detailed history of the Copts, in whose days Egypt presented to the world but a sorry spectacle. Under the pressure of events she was divided into two factions. On the one side were the Copts, who formed a sect that clung all the more closely to their own ideas because the Council of Chalcedon had condemned them ; on the other were the Melkites, a party whom any tie, however small, bound to Constantinople, and who condemned as heretical the opinions of the other half of the nation. These dissensions alone were sufficient to stir up implacable hatred in a society already so much disturbed ; and during the two centuries and a half that followed her religious emancipation, Egypt endured a terrible experience. Riots in the streets, incendiary crimes, organised brigandage in the country—in fact, all the combined horrors of a civil war ; while sanguinary conflicts took place in Alexandria not only between Christians and Jews, but between Christians themselves, who, not being able to agree upon some special point of dogma, attempted to settle it by force of arms. Over the miserable condition of Egypt after the Edict of Theodosius it is not necessary to spend time, though we cannot help adding that the disorder which left such a fatal mark upon this epoch was not attributable to Egypt herself. Under the circumstances it was a great misfortune that she became one of the most important centres of the great political and religious changes that were then agitating the world. From Constantinople—the seat of power—she could only draw examples of the most far-gone corruption. There ' the ostentatious libertinism of the patricians, the servility of the great, the want of discipline of the soldiers, were vices that the great city never attempted to root out. Patriotism gave place to venality and an inordinate thirst for riches. The emperors themselves spent their time—which should have been better employed in the government of the state—in useless theological discussions, and from presiding at their councils would come away to prescribe articles of faith or draw up the inditement of special pleas either for or against the Patriarch's decisions.' [1] Thus in giving way to disorder and revolt, and making religious discussions an every-day occupation, Egypt became engulfed in a torrent that she could not stem. The *rôle* of agitator, whether political or religious, was never suited to Egypt, and

[1] Viennet.

history shows us that every time she attempted it she was forced into it by the events themselves, and not by her own impulse.

Egypt is not a country adapted for such struggles. Her delicious climate, the fertility of the soil, the gentleness of the inhabitants, who are so easily initiated in the ways of civilization, all tend to make her *par excellence* the conservative country. Aggressiveness, the desire for expansion, and propagandism, so common among other races, were, so to speak, unknown in Ancient Egypt, and if outsiders had not come to her and disturbed that tranquillity which was the very essence of her life, it is certain that she would never have gone beyond her own borders to trouble others ; though in a supreme crisis she might perhaps have exerted herself and in her turn become the invader. But these efforts against Nature can only be of short duration ; and we may be sure will only end in a final catastrophe. This is exactly what did happen, after the violent religious disputes above mentioned. Mahomet now appeared, proclaiming another new religion, and Egypt, wearied out with the heavy and undignified yoke of Constantinople, thought to rid herself of it. Makaukes—a Copt of noble birth and immense wealth—undertook the difficult task of regaining for his country her old independence. Being well nigh single-handed against the emperor's soldiers who were shut up in Alexandria, he made overtures to the Arabs, and by means of the promise of annual tribute persuaded Amr'-Ibn-el-Asi, one of Mahomet's lieutenants, to lend him his aid.

Amr' beat the imperial troops, and after a siege of fourteen months entered Alexandria triumphantly. It was in vain that the Byzantines, reinforced by a fleet and a fresh army from Constantinople, won back the city. The Copts, terrified at the idea of again falling under the yoke of the masters whom they thought they had ejected, recalled the Arabs, who, coming to their assistance, again took Alexandria and triumphantly established there the reign of Islam.

The sequel is well known. This time Egypt was neither an independent monarchy as under the Pharaohs, nor a province of the Roman Empire as under the Cæsars, nor even a dependency of the Eastern Empire as under the Byzantine emperors ; she was incorporated into the vast empire of the Khalifs, and became then, and has ever since remained, Moslem. The establishment of Islam, first in Alexandria and afterwards in all the provinces of Egypt, closes the second of the three periods into which the general history of the country is divided.

PART II

APPENDIX

———◦◦◦———

CHAPTER VIII

IN the remarks which formed the introduction to the first chapter of the Heathen Period, the sources from whence our information was drawn were briefly mentioned ; they were—I. the Egyptian monuments themselves ; II. the fragments of Manetho ; III. the Greek and Latin writers.

We must now return to Manetho and the monuments. However long the details concerning these authorities may be, they are very important : to study them is to inquire into our proofs.   It is to ask of Egypt herself the title-deeds of her own history, and at the same time must demonstrate to modern Egyptians the value of those venerable *débris* by which they are surrounded, and which are as precious as the parchment deeds that prove a title of nobility.   Manetho on the one hand, and the monuments on the other, are the two objects with which this Appendix is written.

MANETHO

Under Ptolemy Philadelphus Manetho wrote in Greek a history of Egypt gathered from the official archives preserved in the temples. Like many another history the book itself has disappeared, and we possess to-day but the fragments of it, together with the list of the kings placed originally at the end, which were fortunately preserved in the writings of some of the chroniclers living a few years before the Hegira. This list divides all the sovereigns who reigned over Egypt into dynasties or royal families. For the most part Manetho gives the names of the kings, the lengths of their reigns and the duration of the dynasty ; sometimes, however, he contents himself with briefly touching upon the origin of the royal family, the number of its kings and the number of years during which it reigned. To give these lists completely would stretch this little book to an unnecessary length, but the subjoined are a *résumé* of the principal dynasties which held sway in Egypt.

No one can look at the list of Manetho's dynasties without being struck with the enormous length of time that they occupied : we have in fact to go back to a period that to Egypt is historical, though to most other nations it would be but legendary. Some modern authors, embarrassed by this fact, and not finding any reason for doubting the authenticity and veracity of

No. of Dynasty	Name of Dynasty	Place of Residence
I.	Thinis . .	Harabat-el-Madfûneh .
II.	,, . .	Idem . . . .
III.	Memphis .	Mitrahineh . . .
IV.	,, .	Idem . . . .
V.	,, .	,, ...
VI.	Elephantiné .	Gezireh-Assûan . .
VII.	Memphis .	Mitrahineh . . .
VIII.	,, .	Idem . . . .
IX.	Heracleopolis .	Ahnas-el-Medineh .
X.	,, .	Idem . . . .
XI.	Thebes . .	Medinet Habû . .
XII.	,, . .	Idem . . . .
XIII.	,, . .	,, ...
XIV.	Xoïs . .	Sakha . . .
XV.	Hyksos . .	Sân . . . .
XVI.	,, . .	,, ...
XVII.	,, . .	,, ...

XVIII.	Thebes . .	Medinet Habû . .
XIX.	,, . .	,, ,, . .
XX.	,, . .	,, ,, . .
XXI.	Tanis . .	Sân . . . .
XXII.	Bubastis . .	Tell-Basta . . .
XXIII.	Tanis . .	Sân . . . .
XXIV.	Saïs . .	Sâ-el-Hagar . .
XXV.	Ethiopian .	,, . .
XXVI.	Saïs . .	,, . .
XXVII.	Persian . .	,, . .
XXVIII.	Saïs . .	,, . .
XXIX.	Mendes . .	Ashmûn-er-Rûman .
XXX.	Sebennytes .	Samanhûd . . .
XXXI.	Persian . .	,, . . .

End of Manetho's lis

XXXII.	Macedonian .	. . . . .
XXXIII.	Greek . .	. . . . .
XXXIV.	Roman . .	. . . . .

Edict of Theodosius .

ACCORDING TO MANETHO

Modern Name of Province	Length of Years	Years before Hegira	Years before Christ
Girgeh . .	253	5626	5004
Idem . .	302	5373	4751
Gizeh . .	214	5071	4449
Idem . .	284	4857	4235
,, . .	248	4573	3951
Esneh . .	203	4325	3703
Gizeh . .	70 days	4122	3500
Idem . .	142	4122	3500
Beni Sûef .	109	3980	3358
Idem . .	185	3871	3249
Keneh . .	213	3686	3064
Idem . .	213	3686	3064
,, . .	453	3173	2851
Menufîeh .	184	3020	2398
Sharkîeh .	511	2835	2214
,, .	,,	,,	,,
,, .	,,	,,	,,

Modern Name of Province	Length of Years	Years before Hegira	Years before Christ
Keneh . .	241	2325	1703
,, . .	174	2084	1462
,, . .	178	1910	1288
Sharkîeh .	130	1732	1110
,, .	170	1602	980
,, .	89	1432	810
Gharbîeh .	6	1343	721
,, .	50	1337	715
,, .	138	1287	665
,, .	121	1149	527
,, .	7	1028	406
Dakalîeh .	21	1021	399
Gharbîeh .	38	1000	378
,, .	8	962	340
st.			
. . .	27	954	332
. . .	275	927	305
. . .	411	652	30
			A.D.
. . .		241	381

Manetho, have supposed that Egypt was at different periods divided into more than one kingdom, and that some of the royal families whose reigns were simultaneous have been given as successive. It is, for instance, as if they supposed that the Fifth Dynasty at Elephantiné were contemporaneous with the Sixth at Memphis. It is not necessary to demonstrate the advantages of this system. By drawing some dates closer together, and correcting others, and by an ingenious and clever arrangement of the dynasties, it is possible to shorten almost at will the length of Manetho's list.

Thus it is that where we have in the preceding table B.C. 5004 as the date of the foundation of the Egyptian monarchy, other writers, like Bunsen, place the same event as occurring in B.C. 3623. Which is correct? The more carefully the question is studied, the more difficult appears to be the reply. The greatest of all obstacles to the establishment of an Egyptian chronology lies in the fact that the Egyptians themselves never had one. The use of an era, properly so-called, was unknown to them; and, so far, it cannot yet be proved that they reckoned otherwise than by the years of the reigning monarch. These years were therefore far from having a fixed point of departure; since they were sometimes counted from the death of the late monarch, and sometimes from the coronation of the reigning sovereign. Whatever may be the apparent precision of its calculations, modern science will always be foiled in its attempts to give to Egypt that which she never possessed.

Surrounded as we are by these difficulties, I believe that
the adoption of Manetho's lists in their entirety leads us
nearest to the truth.   Far be it from me to pretend that
from the time of Mena to the emperors Egypt was
always one united kingdom : we may even find out by
unexpected discoveries that there were more collateral
dynasties in this vast empire than even the warmest
partisans of that system would care to admit.   But everything leads to the belief that in Manetho's lists, as they
have come down to us, the work of elimination has
already been done.   If the collateral dynasties had been
given, we ought to find, before or after the Twenty-first
Dynasty, that of the high priests who ruled in Thebes
while the Twenty-first occupied Tanis ; also we must
account for the seven or eight independent kings who were
contemporaneous with the Twenty-third Dynasty, and
who would thus have added—had not Manetho already
eliminated them—as many successive royal families to the
list given by the Egyptian priest.   In the same way the
dodecarchy would count for at least one dynasty, and
must find a place between the Twenty-fifth and Twenty-
sixth ; and the Theban kings themselves, the rivals of the
Hyksos, would have to take their rank before or after the
Seventeenth.   Undoubtedly there were simultaneous
dynasties in Egypt, but Manetho has put them aside, so as
to admit only those reputed to be legitimate ; therefore,
they find no place in his lists.   Were this not the case,
we should have, not thirty-one, but some sixty dynasties

G

between Mena and Alexander. Supposing even that Manetho had not cared to make this elimination himself, we cannot be certain that the abbreviators of Manetho— all more or less interested in diminishing his lists—may not have done so for themselves, as, by possessing the text of the work, they had the means for making the necessary reduction. Everything, then, militates against the system of collateral dynasties ; and for my part I shall not believe in them until I find some instance in which the monuments prove decisively that two royal families, given by Manetho as successive, were simultaneous. In fact, I shall look upon the idea of co-existent dynasties as a pedantic invention, so long as the evidence of the monuments does not establish the theory.

Take, for instance, two examples : First. The greater number of tables give the Fifth Dynasty of Elephantiné as contemporaneous with the Sixth at Memphis. Were this a historic fact, each of these dynasties must have its own special territory, and it would follow that no monument of the Fifth Dynasty would be found upon Sixth Dynasty ground, and *vice versâ*. But the result of our excavations has been the discovery of Fifth Dynasty monuments both at Elephantiné and at Sakkarah ; and again of Sixth Dynasty monuments at Sakkarah and at Elephantiné. Second. The Fourteenth Dynasty of Xoïs would be reigning at the same time as the Thirteenth at Thebes ; but the Thirteenth Dynasty colossi found at Sân

—only a few miles from Sakha—prove that the Theban Dynasty who erected them possessed Lower Egypt. These details alone show that there is much to be said against the system of collateral dynasties about whom Science has not said yet her last word. Undoubtedly in matters of detail many of the figures stand in need of correction, but I maintain that in the thirty-one dynasties of Manetho we have—without the admission of collateral dynasties—the series of legitimate and successive royal families, according to the official registers, up to the time of Alexander. Here let us leave the question of dates, strictly speaking, with regard to which I can only repeat what I have elsewhere said : [1] 'As to assigning a fixed date to each of the royal families, and therefore to their contemporaneous monuments, I would remind you that until the time of Psammetichus I. Dynasty XXVI., B.C. 665, it is impossible to do more than give approximate figures, which become still less certain as we go backwards into the ages. No one has yet succeeded in conquering the difficulties of Egyptian chronology.

' The method of reckoning by the years of the reigning monarch has always been an obstacle to the establishment of a fixed calendar, and there is nothing by which to prove that the Egyptians ever made use of an era properly so called. Here again Manetho is our best guide, though, unfortunately, a single glance at those portions of his history preserved in the works of Christian

---

[1] *Introduction de la Notice Sommaire du Musée de Búlaq.*

writers is sufficient to show evidences of both carelessness and wilful alteration.   Proper names are often defaced, sometimes even transposed ; and figures vary as
the extract in question is given according to Eusebius or
to Africanus.   Also, the totals given at the end of each
dynasty are rarely in accordance with the sum of the
reigns comprehended within that dynasty.   Manetho's
lists have come down to us in such a condition that we
shall never be able to fix our dates definitely by them.
I know that there are some people who, by attaching
certain undisputed synchronisms to Manetho's lists, have
thus attempted to restore their chronological use, and
the method in itself ought to be infallible.   Being given,
for instance, the heliacal rising of Sirius on a certain
date in a certain year of a king's reign mentioned by
Manetho, it is clear that by a calculation easy enough to
astronomers the Julian year, the date of the phenomenon,
and that of the monarch's reign, could all be determined.
In this direction Science has gone to her furthest limits,
as the works of M. Biot and M. de Rougé will show.
But in order that these results may never be questioned,
it is first of all necessary that we should be quite sure,
when giving the rising of a certain star as the occasion of
one of the temple fêtes, that the Egyptians meant a
rising accurately observed ; and secondly, this having
been ascertained, we must be equally sure that they were
able at that period to triumph over the uncertainty of all
observations made without the aid of instruments.   On

this last point see M. Biot's remarks on what he calls his
"scientific puritanism." The Biblical and Assyrian synchronisms, by means of which it was hoped to be able to
verify Manetho's lists, are but of little use. That Moses
lived under Ramses II., and that Merenptah was the
Pharaoh of the Exodus, are facts already acknowledged
by science, but they afford us no help as to the chronology of the Nineteenth Dynasty; for the Biblical data
may lead to contradictory inferences concerning the
duration of the Judges, and consequently as to the epoch
that saw Moses set himself at the head of the Hebrew
people. We are met by equally great difficulties in
attempting to assign a date to the synchronism of the
capture of Jerusalem by Shishak, the first king of the
Twenty-second Dynasty; for from the book of the Kings
we get no nearer to a definite date than that in a certain
year of Shishak's reign he invaded Jerusalem. We must
come down to the Twenty-sixth Dynasty for the limit of
exact chronology (B.C. 665). It is quite impossible to
give back to Manetho's lists the chronological accuracy
of which the alterations of copyists have deprived them;
and it must be recognised that, although the science of
to-day feels equal to affirming that a given monument
belongs to a particular dynasty, it must nevertheless
refuse to date the period to which that monument belongs. The further the period is removed from our own
era, the greater becomes the difficulty; so much so, that
among the various systems of Egyptology, it is possible

to differ by 2,000 years as to the age of the foundation
of the Egyptian monarchy.'²

						B.C.
² Boeckh gives	.	.	.	.	.	5702
Unger	.	.	.	.	.	5613
Mariette and Lenormant		.	.	.	.	5004
Maspero	.	.	.	.	.	4500
Brugsch	.	.	.	.	.	4455
Lauth	.	.	.	.	.	4157
Lepsius and Ebers		.	.	.	.	3892
Bunsen	.	.	.	.	.	3623
Birch .	.	.	.	.	.	3000
R. S. Poole	.	.	.	.	.	2717
Gardiner Wilkinson		.	.	.	.	2691

A difference of 3,011 years !

CHAPTER IX

THE MONUMENTS

THERE is not any country besides Egypt whose history can be written on the testimony of so many original proofs. Egyptian monuments are to be found not only in the country itself, but even in Nubia, the Sûdan, and so far away as Beyrût. To these, already very numerous, must be added the quantities of antique objects that during the last fifty years have been passing into Europe to enrich the collections possessed by nearly every capital. To make known the principal monuments, and their connection with the history of Egypt, is the object of this chapter ; and I shall speak first of those monuments which are of general interest in history, and then of those which by belonging to one particular dynasty serve to lay it open to us and give proof in detail, so to say, of its existence.

The principal monuments which are of general interest to the history of Egypt are the following : First, a papyrus which was sold to the Turin Museum by M. Drovetti, the Consul-General of France, and which is there preserved. If only it were intact, no monument would be

more precious.   In it is to be found a list of all the personages, both mythical and historical, who have reigned
over Egypt from fabulous times until an epoch that—
since we do not possess the end of the papyrus—we cannot ascertain.   Drawn up under Ramses II., that is to
say, at one of the best epochs of Egyptian history, this
list carries all the weight of an official document, and if
perfect would be most valuable, in that the name of
every king is followed by the length of his reign, and
that to every dynasty has been added the total number
of years during which it governed the affairs of Egypt.
Unfortunately, the carelessness of the fellahin who discovered it, and, worse still, the negligence of those who
brought it into Europe, have been the destruction of the
Royal Papyrus of Turin, and this invaluable treasure has
been so roughly handled that it only exists now in minute
fragments (about 164), which it is impossible to piece
together again.   From being of incomparable value, it is
therefore now but little credited, and seldom even quoted
in works upon Egyptology.

Secondly, another valuable monument which has been
taken away from the temple at Karnak by M. Prisse and
presented to the Bibliothèque Nationale in Paris.   It is
a small chamber, upon the walls of which Thothmes III.
may be seen making offerings to sixty-one of his predecessors—hence its name, the Hall of Ancestors.   But
it is not a regular and uninterrupted series of the kings,
for Thothmes III. has made a selection before whom to
pay his respects, though what may have been the reason

of his choice is entirely unknown to us. At first sight we can only look upon the Hall of Ancestors as an extract from the list of Egyptian royalties. The compiler, from motives quite unknown to us, has taken the names of the kings indiscriminately, sometimes giving an entire dynasty, at others leaving out long periods. Besides that, the artist entrusted with the ornamentation of the room has done it from the point of view of decoration only, and not troubled himself to place the figures in chronological order. Owing to most unfortunate injuries which this monument has sustained (twelve royal names are missing), the Paris table of the kings loses much of its importance. So that, taking it altogether, the Hall of Ancestors has not given to science as much help as was anticipated. However, it has rendered invaluable service in determining better than any other list the names of the Thirteenth Dynasty kings.

To the above-named monuments must be added the Table of Abydos. As may be gathered from its name, it came from that site, being brought away by M. Mimaut, Consul-General of France; it is now in the British Museum. Of all the innumerable Egyptian monuments, there is not one that is so famous, nor that less deserves its fame. This time it is Ramses II. who adores his ancestors, and out of the fifty cartouches— besides that of Ramses repeated twenty-eight times— there are now but thirty left, and these are in a state more or less incomplete. Like the Hall of Ancestors, the Table of Abydos gives a list resulting from the artist's choice, the reason of which is also unknown. Another fact that depreciates its value is that we do not possess its commencement. After the Twelfth Dynasty, however, the list passes at once without a break to the Eighteenth. But to what dynasties are we to assign the fourteen unknown cartouches placed before the Twelfth? Do they belong to the more ancient of the royal families, or do they but serve to fill up the gap between the Sixth and the Eleventh Dynasties? Unlike the Turin Papyrus, the Table of Abydos could never have been one of the foundation stones of Egyptology, though in the early days of that science it undoubtedly helped Champollion in the classification of the Eighteenth Dynasty kings, and later on it served Lepsius as a landmark in arranging the Amen-em-hats and Usertsens, and in identifying them with the kings of Manetho's Twelfth Dynasty. Beyond this, however, the Table of Abydos is useless, and it is not likely that it will ever disclose any of those startling facts which have proved so useful to the progress of Egyptological science.[1]

The most interesting, as also the most perfect monu-

[1] There are two temples at Abydos dedicated to the local divinity : the one built by Seti, the other by Ramses. The same series of kings, twice repeated without any variation, adorns these buildings. One is the Table described above, the other was discovered comparatively lately. Although in an admirable state of preservation, this tablet adds but little to our knowledge. It mentions some new kings, and shows the correct sequence of others, but is far from giving us a connected series of all the kings of Egypt from Menes to Seti I.—MARIETTE.

ment of this kind, is the one that was found during the French excavations at Sakkarah, and which is now in the Gizeh Palace. Unlike the others, it is not of royal origin. It was discovered in the tomb of an Egyptian priest named Tunari, who lived in the days of Ramses II. According to the Egyptian belief, one of the good things reserved for the dead who were deemed worthy of eternal life was to be admitted to the society of their kings, and Tunari is represented as having been received into the august assembly of fifty-eight. Here again in the Tablet of Sakkarah, as before in that of Abydos, is raised the same question : Why these fifty-eight kings more than any others ? Until it has been answered, the Tablet of Sakkarah can only be allowed a relative authority. It must be granted, however, that the list in the Gizeh Palace possesses unquestionable advantages. In the first place we have the beginning of it, and thus can start from a definite point ; in the second place, between the beginning and the end of the series are added other already known cartouches which form intermediary land-marks, and give to the whole a precision not found in the other documents. Before the Eighteenth, Twelfth, and Eleventh Dynasties we come to the first six, and they are (unhoped-for good fortune) almost as complete in the Tablet of Sakkarah as in the list of Manetho.[2]

[2] The Tablet of Sakkarah does not mention the first kings of Egypt. M. Mariette does not do justice to the great Tablet of Abydos in his mention of it in the preceding note. M. de Rougé describes it as ' a new list of the Pharaohs, more com-

These are the most celebrated monuments bearing general interest on Egyptian history. Now we will take the dynasties of Manetho one by one, and point out the principal monuments belonging to each of them. But before proceeding with this novel inventory let me remind you that Egyptology is a new-born science, and a history of Egypt cannot be written, as that of most other countries can be, by following along a beaten track with one's eyes half closed. At every step we have to reconnoitre the path, and while slowly making our way along it, have at the same time to collect and register all the landmarks, and then gather together the materials picked up here and there, just as a clever workman pieces the thousand-and-one fragments of a precious vase long since broken. You will not be surprised then if, instead of always going straight on to the end, we linger sometimes over details which in any other case would be useless; neither will you be surprised if, for the sake of proving the value of such investigations, we make you take part

plete and more important than any of those we previously possessed. King Seti I., accompanied by his son Ramses, renders homage in it to seventy-six sovereigns, selected from his predecessors from the time of Menes. In this enormous list only two or three names have been slightly altered. Another fact makes it still more precious; the order of the kings has been found strictly historical wherever the authority of monuments has allowed the opportunity of verification. We may, therefore, consider the new Tablet of Seti I. as free from those artificial groups, and from those irregularities which occasion so much trouble to us in our interpretations of the lists of Karnak, and even of Sakkarah.'
—*Monuments qu'on peut attribuer aux six premières Dynasties*, p. 14 and following.

from time to time in some of those tedious processes by which we are striving to build up little by little the fabric of Ancient Egyptian History.

FIRST, SECOND, AND THIRD DYNASTIES

Manetho is our guide for the reconstruction of these three dynasties ; but of necessity he must be followed with caution on account of the remoteness of the period with which he deals. Fortunately the Tablet of Sakkarah comes to the help of the Egyptian annalist ; but as it gives only a selection of the kings, we must not expect to find on it all the names that are given in Manetho. However, it cites two kings of the First Dynasty, six of the Second, and eight of the Third. This is enough to show that the historian reported correctly the Egyptian tables. From henceforth we may assert that Manetho's first three dynasties belong to the authentic history of Egypt, and we may go even further and say that neither of them was contemporary with the other. In spite of their extreme antiquity, the monuments of those dynasties are still fairly numerous. The most ancient of them is the Step Pyramid of Sakkarah, which dates back to the fourth king of the First Dynasty.[3] After that comes the tomb

---

[3] According to Manetho 'he' (Unenephes) built the pyramid at Cochome ; Cochome being the Greek form of Ka-kam, *i.e.* the black bull, which, according to the stelæ and sarcophagi of the Serapēum, was in the neighbourhood of Sakkarah.

of Ptah-hotep discovered at Sakkarah and still in place ;[4]
then the three statues of the Sepa functionaries found at
the Pyramids and now in the Louvre ;[5] and finally the
statue of Amten, who was contemporaneous with the last
but one king of the Third Dynasty, and which was taken
from the Pyramids to Berlin by Lepsius.

FOURTH AND FIFTH DYNASTIES

Manetho and the Tablet of Sakkarah are again our
chief authorities for the arrangement of the kings of this
period, and their accounts run together so closely that it
is evident that the two lists have a common origin, and
it is therefore the strongest confirmation, given as yet by
the monuments, of the veracity of Manetho and his
table of the Ancient Empire. Those of this period
are the best known perhaps of any in Egypt. I have
before spoken of the Pyramids.[6] Those of Gizeh belong
strictly to the Fourth ; amongst the others those of
Abûsîr, extending into the Fifth, should be specially
noticed, while the magnificent tombs found at the Pyramids and at Sakkarah furnish us with important specimens

[4] Ptah-hotep was a priest of
the Pyramids of Aser, Ra-en-
user and the 'divine dwelling
of Men-kau-Hor,' and lived in
the Fifth Dynasty.

[5] Two of these statues belong to Sepa, who is described
as ' prophet and priest of the
White Bull ;' the third is the
figure of Nesa, a relation of the
king's, and possibly wife of
Sepa.

[6] That of Mêdûm belongs
to King Sneferu of the Third
Dynasty.

of the civilization of the country under those two royal families. To this list must also be added the great alabaster and granite temple discovered close to the Sphinx, which is quite unique at present, since it is the only specimen we have of the monumental architecture of the Ancient Empire.[7]

Then in the Gizeh Palace we have as the chief objects of this epoch [8]—

The statue of Khafra, the builder of the Second Pyramid, which is remarkable not only for its great age —sixty centuries at least—but for its breadth and majesty, as well as for the finish of its details. It is, therefore, a rare object. It also throws an unexpected light across the history of Egyptian Art, and shows that six thousand years ago the Egyptian artist had but little more progress to make.

An inscription carved upon a square stone and dating back to the time of Khufu, the builder of the Great Pyramid. It relates to offerings made by him to a temple, which consisted of sacred images in stone, gold, bronze, ivory, and wood. This inscription is valuable as a model

---

[7] In 1891 the temple of King Sneferu was discovered adjoining the east face of the Pyramid of Mêdûm. It is a perfect specimen of a pyramid temple; but owing to the total absence of official conservation it was re-buried in order to preserve it.

[8] Two beautiful limestone statues from Mêdûm, representing Ra-hotep and his sister or wife, Nefert. They belong to the end of the Third Dynasty.

A group of geese feeding, found in a ruined mastaba at the same place. They are executed in water colours on plaster, and are most life-like.

of the monumental formulæ of the Fourth Dynasty, and stands in the same relation to language and writing as the statue of Khafra does to sculpture. It determines also the condition of Egyptian civilization at that epoch, and furnishes us at the same time with a standard of comparison according to which may be classified the monuments belonging to the different periods of the Ancient Empire.

A great stela found at the Pyramids of Gizeh, and dedicated to the memory of a princess who, after having been ' great favourite '[9] in the courts of Sneferu and Khufu, was subsequently attached to the private house of Khafra. This stela determines the relative sequence of those three Pharaohs, which is in accordance with Manetho's list.

A wooden statue ; and never has Egyptian art produced so striking a portrait. The head specially has been executed in the most life-like manner ; the features are of the small rounded type that one meets nowadays in most of the villages of Lower Egypt, and those at their very best. It must have been more remarkable still when covered with that fine coating of stucco laid upon gauze with which the sculptor finished his work.[1]

Several fine sarcophagi of both rose and black granite.

---

[9] On the title of ' Great Favourite,' see p. 8 of paper on ' The Priestly Character of the Earliest Egyptian Civilization,' by P. le Page Renouf, in *Pro-* *ceedings of the Soc. Bib. Arch.* for May, 1890.

[1] Known as the Shêkh-el-Belled, or Wooden Man of Bûlaq.

The former belonged to princes of the Fourth Dynasty, the latter are valuable on account of the ornamentations with which the four external faces are covered. They are excellent models of that bold architecture used in the façades of Fourth Dynasty buildings. There are also a large number of monolithic stelæ belonging to this period. The Gizeh Palace alone possesses about fifty of them

SIXTH DYNASTY

Four kings according to the Tablet of Sakkarah, six according to Manetho : the former gives thirty-six names since Mena, the latter forty-nine ; while the six dynasties have their representatives elsewhere on the stela of Tunari. From this I conclude unhesitatingly that there is no collateral family among them. The monuments of the Sixth Dynasty are to be found at Elephantiné, El-Kab, Kasr-es-Syad, Abydos, Shêkh Saïd, Zawit-el-Mytin, Memphis, Sân, and Wady Magharah. It therefore possessed the Nile country from the Mediterranean to the Cataract. Among the monuments of this dynasty now in the Gizeh Palace there are—   .

First. A long inscription of fifty lines, coming from a tomb at Abydos, in which Una, a functionary, relates his history. After having gained several honours under Teta and Pepi, he served under a third king named Mer-en-Ra. This tablet announces the curious fact that Pepi (*Apappus*) reigned a hundred years, while it gives a

H

chronological sequence of the three kings, Teta, Pepi, and Mer-en-Ra.[2]

Secondly. An inscription relating to another functionary of Abydos, who began his life under Pepi and Mer-en-Ra, and finally died under a fourth Pharaoh named Nefer-ka-Ra. So by comparing together these two stelæ of Abydos we make sure of the succession of four of the Sixth Dynasty kings. And this furnishes a very good example of the methods by which science is patiently striving to place each one of the long line of Egyptian kings in his own place. Before finishing with the monuments of the first three dynasties, I want to point out to you the principal characteristics of these extremely ancient relics. First, they nearly all have a common object : they are funerary. The tombs themselves are for the most part built upon a uniform plan. A massive square construction wherein, on fixed anniversaries, the relatives of the deceased may assemble ; a shaft sunk vertically into the ground, and at the bottom of the shaft a chamber in which could be for ever sealed up the remains of the defunct ; such is their general arrangement. The method of their adornment is nearly as uniform. More figures than text ; an entire absence of all representations of the gods ; numberless scenes taken from private life, and relating particularly to agriculture ; the religious titles of the deceased rather than his civil ones ; and the frequent use of royal

---

[2] An English translation of the tablet of Una may be found in *Records of the Past*, vol. ii. p. 1 *et seq.*

cartouches, are the chief characteristics ; the sculpture being at the same time vigorous, yet refined. Still there are differences in these monuments, which allow of our dividing them into three classes. The first belongs to the most ancient type of all, such as the tomb of Amten. There we feel that both writing and art are but in process of formation. The hieroglyphs are scattered and in relief, the outlines are rough, and the figures stumpy, while their anatomical details are exaggerated. The second style is more shapely ; the hieroglyphs are not so harsh, and there is more harmony in their arrangements. The texts themselves are better. The syllabic signs which form the greater part of the inscriptions of the time of Amten are found to be gradually giving way to the alphabetic : there are fewer pedigrees, and the formula of invocation is addressed to Anubis alone. The tomb of Ti at Sakkarah is the best example that I know of belonging to this period.[3] The third belongs to the Sixth Dynasty ; the name of Osiris, hitherto rarely used, becomes more frequent ; the formula of ' the justified ' is occasionally met with ; the texts become longer, and long prayers and biographical details vary the monotony

[3] Ti was a functionary in the service of Ra-nefer-ar-ka, Ra-en-user, and Kaka, all kings of the Fifth Dynasty ; with the dignities of ' master of the secrets,' ' president of the gate of the palace,' and ' secret counsellor of the king in all his royal assemblies,' he combined also the religious offices of ' chief of the prophets,' ' president of the sacrifices of purification,' and ' guardian of the mystery of the divine speech.'

The various scenes from the tomb of Ti have been admirably photographed from impressions by Dr. Reil.

of the representations.   It is in the tombs of this period, and of the time of Ti, that have been found those statues of slender build, with round faces, smiling lips, refined noses, square shoulders, and muscular limbs, of which the Gizeh Palace possesses not a few.   It is also from these same sepulchres that those large monolithic stelæ, shaped like the façade of a building, come.   But for how long a period subsequent to the Sixth Dynasty these monuments were in fashion we do not know.   I have long tried to find in the necropolis of Sakkarah a solution of the following twofold problem.   Are we to regard these last-mentioned tombs as posterior to the Sixth Dynasty, or even contemporaneous with the Twelfth, which curiously enough is not represented at all in the cemetery at Memphis?   Or in the face of those Theban monuments of Eleventh Dynasty work, which are totally different in style, must we suppose that the burial traditions of Ancient Egypt had been suddenly broken into, during those hitherto unexplained disturbances which, following upon the Sixth Dynasty, have left the monumental void before alluded to?   As yet we have not any grounds for forming a definite judgment.

SEVENTH, EIGHTH, NINTH, AND TENTH DYNASTIES

The absence of monuments is one of the distinguishing features of this period.   There is, however, nothing surprising in the fact of finding several tombs bearing the cartouches of Pepi and Teta and other Memphite kings belonging to the first two of these four dynasties. We have as yet found no traces of the Ninth and Tenth Dynasties, which Manetho places at Heracleopolis: possibly because Mêdûm, Licht, Ahnas-el-Medineh, and all the district at the entrance of the Fayûm have been neglected by excavators.[4] Perhaps the fourteen cartouches in the upper row of the Table of Abydos may represent the kings of this very epoch, or it may be that some of those personages belonging to the blood royal, who figure in the Hall of Ancestors, may have profited by the troublous times to pave the way for the accession of the Eleventh Dynasty; in which case they would, of course, be contemporaneous with the Tenth. Further monuments are, however, indispensable for settling the question as to whether some of the Sebek-hoteps did not belong to the Seventh, Eighth, Ninth, or Tenth Dynasty. We must wait for further excavations for the thorough study of this period.

ELEVENTH DYNASTY

Manetho does not give the names of the kings composing this dynasty; but the monuments supply us with half a dozen who probably all belonged to one family, but who for long remained unclassified. A stela in the Leyden Museum determines our knowledge of their

---

[4] Since the above was written Mr. Petrie has spent some time excavating in the Fayûm. See his volumes on Kahun and Hawâra, and the Egypt Exploration Fund Report on Ahnas.

position in the Egyptian annals. From the text en graven upon it we gather that an individual who died under a king already known to be of the Twelfth Dynasty had for his great-grandfather a man who lived under one of the kings of this very group. It is therefore impossible to doubt that these kings of a dynasty preceding the Twelfth must have formed the Eleventh. We must excavate at Drah-abû'l-neggah, a district of Thebes, in order to obtain further information concerning it. Already the fellahin have found there, for many years past, both rare and valuable objects which can only have come from royal tombs, but, unfortunately, having fallen into the hands of ignorant people, they have been but of little use to science. There are in the Gizeh Palace, as the result of the French excavations in that locality, several stelæ; and nearly all the specimens of vases, fruits, bread, clothing, furniture, arms, and utensils of all kinds come from there. In drawing up the history of the Eleventh Dynasty I spoke of the rude style which is one of the characteristics of this epoch, and I would have you observe that the objects belonging to it do not in the least resemble those of the preceding dynasties. What- ever may have been the causes, the Eleventh Dynasty was a period of renaissance. The stelæ, instead of being square, are now rounded at the top. The hieroglyphs have their own individual clumsiness, which is quite unlike that of the Third Dynasty tombs. At first sight even one notices a difference in the sarcophagi; and in allusion to Isis, who extends her wings over Osiris—to whom the dead is likened—and thus protects him, the coffins are covered with wings painted in brilliant and varied colours. As before stated, Manetho only briefly mentions the Eleventh Dynasty, and does not name the kings. The Tablet of Sakkarah gives but two cartouches, while the Hall of Ancestors—if only the artist had not arranged the cartouches anyhow, i.e. Eleventh Dynasty kings mixed up with Sixth and Twelfth with Seventeenth, would have been by far the most complete list. There is much to be discovered concerning this interesting dynasty, whose remains must be sought for at Drah-abû'l-neggah.

[In 1885, M. Maspero suggested that the Siût tombs were of the period of Heracleopolite kings (Dynasties IX. and X.) Since 1887, Mr. F. Ll. Griffith has been carefully examining and copying the inscriptions from these tombs, with the following interesting historical results. That the princes Kheti I., T'efaba, and Kheti II. were probably contemporary with the close of the Ninth Dynasty or beginning of the Tenth, and that there is evidence to show the existence of hostile feeling between Heracleopolis and Thebes ; the magnates of Siût siding with the former princes. Also Mr. Griffith points out the cartouche of a certain Ra-neb-kau, mentioned in the Papyrus No. ii., Berlin, as probably belonging to the Ninth or Tenth Dynasty. See the inscriptions of Siût and Dêr Rîfeh by F. Ll. Griffith.]

TWELFTH DYNASTY.

This dynasty is composed of the two families of Usertsen and Amen-em-hat. The list of them is to be found not only in Manetho, but in the Table of Abydos, the Tablet of Sakkarah, and the Hall of Ancestors. At Wady Magharah, and at Semneh and Kumneh (above Wady Halfah), are traces of them ; to them we owe the obelisks of Matarîyeh, near Cairo, and Begig in the Fayûm ; the magnificent hypogea of Beni-Hasan, some of the grottoes at Siût, and several grand colossi found at Sân and Abydos. All these are remarkable for the dignity of their style, and prove that one of the most brilliant epochs of Egyptian art was that which was contemporaneous with the Twelfth Dynasty. For long this dynasty's exact place in the series was uncertain, and in the early days of Egyptology the Table of Abydos was the only means whereby its chronological position could even be suggested. There is now no doubt that the Table of Abydos, in placing Usertsen next to the Thothmes (Eighteenth Dynasty), skipped over five dynasties, thus making, with apparently good reason, the Usertsens belong to the Seventeenth Dynasty. It was Lepsius who first discovered this mistake. Manetho gives to the Twelfth Dynasty a list of kings among whom the names of Amenemes and Sesortis predominate ; the Table, on the other hand, mentions a number of sovereigns all of whom were either Usertsen or Amen-em-hat. The series of Abydos names adapts itself, with correction, to those of the national historian. The Usertsens are not the Seventeenth Dynasty, and the above short explanation is enough to show that their place is undoubtedly among the Twelfth Dynasty kings. There is yet another fact to be mentioned ; Manetho reckons the Twelfth Dynasty to have lasted for 160 years, and the Eleventh 43, making a total of 203 years. The papyrus of Turin gives 213 years as the length of one royal family, which was terminated by the two last kings of the Twelfth Dynasty, but whose commencement has been lost, owing to the mutilated condition of the text. May we correct the error of the ten years in Manetho, and carry those 213 years over both the Eleventh and Twelfth Dynasties, which the papyrus seems to have counted as one? The answer is made more uncertain inasmuch as at Drah-abû'l-neggah has been found a stela on which is given the fiftieth year of the reign of a king of that dynasty, which, according to Manetho, lasted only forty-three years.

THIRTEENTH AND FOURTEENTH DYNASTIES

Manetho does not give the names of the kings in either of these dynasties, a fact which adds to our difficulties when trying to reconstruct the corresponding monumental series. However, the monuments themselves help us somewhat. On the right-hand side of the Hall of Ancestors, and also on divers objects preserved in various museums, may be read the names of several Pharaohs, all of whom were more or less Sebek-hoteps or Nefer-hoteps, and who seem to form a large family to themselves. Where are they to be placed? An inscription at Semneh described by M. de Rougé mentions Sebek-hotep I. *as living*, and Usertsen III. *as dead*, therefore the Sebek-hoteps are posterior to the Twelfth Dynasty. The Turin Papyrus also furnishes similar information. Fortunately a large piece of it containing the upper part of two columns has been preserved ; on the first column are some well-known cartouches of the Twelfth Dynasty, while the second begins with the pre-nomen-cartouche of Sebek-hotep IV., which is another proof that the large family bearing the name of this last monarch must follow those of the Amen-em-hats and Usertsens. It must also be remembered, first, that the Sebek-hoteps are anterior to the Eighteenth Dynasty, since it is a monument of the time of Thothmes III. that makes them known to us. Secondly, that they were independent kings possessing Egypt from the Mediterranean Sea to the south of Nubia, therefore they cannot have been contemporaneous with the Hyksos, who formed the Fifteenth, Sixteenth, and Seventeenth Dynasties. Our margin of possible errors is therefore becoming more and more contracted, and our only doubt now lies between the Thirteenth and the Fourteenth Dynasty. But the Thirteenth Dynasty lasted 453 years, and had Thebes for its capital ; therefore it is more likely that those fine monuments of the Sebek-hoteps are due to it rather than to the Fourteenth Dynasty, which lasted but 184 years, and reigned from an obscure locality in the Delta (Xoïs).

It is in vain that Manetho passes over in silence the
kings who succeeded Amenemes and Sesortis, for Science
by a series of subtle and ingenious inductions knows how
to recover them. Not only in the Turin Papyrus and on
the right-hand side of the Hall of Ancestors do we meet
with these two dynasties, but their cartouches may be
found scattered about on stelæ in several museums, on
the columns at Sân, and on the walls of some of the
hypogea of Siût, as well as at Assûan and Hammamât.
There are in the Gizeh Palace some cartouches—amongst
them that of a Skhaï-het—which are conjecturally classed
as belonging to the Fourteenth Dynasty, but I should
not be surprised were fresh researches and newly-found
monuments to oblige us to place these kings as far back
as the period between the Sixth and Eleventh Dynasties.

FIFTEENTH AND SIXTEENTH DYNASTIES

The Hyksos invasion is the cause of the absence of
all monuments of this period. These people have left
no traces of their arrival in Egypt, and it is possible that
the native kings, expelled from the eastern provinces of
the Delta, may still have reigned in some hitherto unknown locality in Upper Egypt, but they, no more than
the Hyksos, are represented in the series of Egyptian
monuments.

SEVENTEENTH DYNASTY

A double dynasty consisting of the Hyksos rulers at
Sân and the Egyptian kings at Thebes. The renaissance

which now took place at Thebes is curiously analogous
to that which marked the accession of the Eleventh
Dynasty.   Drah-abû'l-neggah became from this time the
new cemetery of Thebes.   The 'feather-pattern' coffins
containing badly-made mummies reappeared, and the
tombs are found to contain the same vases, the same
weapons, and the same furniture.   Some of the coffins
belonging to princely and other personages of high rank,
besides being adorned with the traditional wings, are
gilded from head to foot, the play of colour caused by
the gold on the raised parts being a reminder of one of
the legends of Isis when protecting Osiris, 'she has caused
light by her wings.'   Again do we find the names of
Entef, Ameni, Aahmes, and Aah-hotep, and it is difficult
for even the most practised eye to distinguish between
these monuments and those belonging to a period long
anterior to the Hyksos invasion.   We find the names of
the Seventeenth Dynasty kings and princes in the lists
on the walls of certain hypogea at Gûrnah, on a libation
table in the Marseilles Museum, on several objects preserved in the great public collections in Europe, and in
the Gizeh Palace.   The abbreviators of Manetho have
left us his divers lists of kings forming the Seventeenth
Dynasty of Sân, in whose proper names (Saïtes, Staan,
Assis, Asseth, Sethos) that of the god Set (Sutekh), a
divinity reverenced chiefly by the Khetas, seems to have
been embodied.   Two names only of the Seventeenth
Dynasty kings have hitherto been found on the monu-
,ments ; one is that of Saïtes, the first king, and the other,

Apōphis, the last; the Egyptian method of writing his name (Apapi) corresponds exactly with Apappus, a king of the Sixth Dynasty. The monuments belonging to the Hyksos of the Seventeenth Dynasty are—

First. Four large Sphinxes found at Sân, which instead of the ordinary head-dress have a thick lion's mane; the features are angular, severe and strongly marked, reminding one forcibly of those of the fisher-folk on Lake Menzaleh; upon the right shoulder of one of them Apōphis has engraved his cartouches, adding to them the further title of 'Beloved of Set.' Later on, Merenptah, of the Nineteenth Dynasty, usurped them, as did also Psousennes, of the Twenty-first.

Second. A granite group, consisting of two persons standing upright, supporting on their outstretched hands a table of offerings covered with fish and flowers: this magnificent work has nothing engraved upon it, but the heads, which are identical with those of the four Sphinxes, fix its date.

Third. The head of a Hyksos king found at Mit-Fares in the Fayûm; an important discovery, and one which shows that the Shepherds had been as far south as this, and consequently had occupied Memphis. Also a colossal black granite head of a king from Bubastis.

Fourth. A papyrus now in the British Museum, according to which Sekenen-Ra governed at Thebes while Apōphis was established at Sân. This papyrus also tells of a quarrel between the two sovereigns, and we gain from it a foresight of coming hostilities.[5]

Fifth. A second account engraved on the tomb of a functionary named Aahmes at El-Kab, and descriptive of the principal events in his life. His youth was passed under Sekenen-Ra, and afterwards he took part in those campaigns of Aahmes against the Hyksos which resulted in their expulsion.

Sixth. And belonging only indirectly to the Seventeenth Dynasty of the Hyksos is the great granite stela found at Sân. It belongs really to the reign of Ramses II. (Nineteenth Dynasty), and dates from the year 400 of King 'Set-aa-pehti-Nubti.'[6] If this king is the Saïtes of Manetho, it would seem, whatever be the object of the stela, that 400 years had elapsed between the accession of the Seventeenth Dynasty and that year of Ramses II.'s reign in which this text was inscribed. This intelligence is, of course, of the utmost importance chronologically. It is true that the particular year of the king's reign is unknown, but since the stela contains an invocation to Set, and the worship of Set (Sutekh) was not re-established in Sân until after the peace between Ramses and the Khetas was concluded in the twenty-third year of Ramses' reign, it follows

[5] The Sallier Papyrus. There are English translations by E. L. Lushington in *Trans. Bib. Arch. Soc.*, vol. iv. p. 263, and in *Records of the Past*, vol. viii. p. 1 *et seq.*

[6] For a more modern reading of this name see 'Bubastis,' p. 21 *et seq.*, vol. viii. of *Publications of the Egypt Exploration Fund.*

that the date must be posterior to the above-named event.[7]

[Seventh. Two very fine colossal statues in black granite found at Bubastis; unfortunately neither of them is perfect. The head and fragment of one statue is in the Gizeh Palace ; the other, which is nearly complete, is in the British Museum. On both faces are clearly depicted the special characteristics of the Hyksos type, although the two portraits are not identical. It is impossible to determine who they represent; the base of the Gizeh statue showing two erasures, while the one in the British Museum has had the name of the owner most carefully chiselled out. Both have been usurped by Osorkon II., and the one in the Gizeh Palace by Ramses II. as well.]

EIGHTEENTH DYNASTY

It is not without difficulty that the kings of this dynasty have been classed. Most unfortunate alterations cause doubts to be thrown upon Manetho's list ; for the proper names in it have been badly transcribed, and some of the reigns have even been transposed. The Table of Abydos, which alone of the hieroglyphic monuments has preserved a list of the kings in sequence, is not complete, and in some places has purposely

[7] For further information concerning the monuments of Sân, see vols. ii. and v. of *Publications of the Egypt Exploration Fund.*

omitted certain royal personages, whom doubtless it considered as illegitimate. As to the Tablet of Sakkarah, out of twelve cartouches placed between Amosis and Ramses II., ten are irretrievably lost. We must, therefore, give up all hope of finding a list of the kings of the Eighteenth Dynasty either in Manetho or on the monuments, and we must compile it as best we can from the result of our study of the texts. Chief amongst these are—

First. The inscription of El-Kab, wherein, as has before been said, we find the four kings under whom Aahmes lived chronologically given—Sekenen-Ra, Amosis, Amenophis I., and Thothmes I.[8] The first of these monarchs belonged to the end of the Seventeenth Dynasty, the other three head the Eighteenth.[9]

Second. Another inscription, also taken from a tomb at El-Kab, and the base of a statue discovered in the same tomb, and now in the Louvre. The person to whom these two last monuments belonged lived successively under Amosis, Amenophis I., Thothmes I., Thothmes II., and Thothmes III. In the course of the inscription Hatshepsu, the queen-regent, is mentioned, but not placed chronologically ; however, as Thothmes III. erased her cartouches, and she constantly did the same by those of Thothmes II., it follows that

[8] English translation by P. le Page Renouf in *Records of the Past*, vol. vi. p. 5.

[9] From the study of Queen Aah-hotep's jewellery there is reason to believe that a king named Kames came between Sekenen-Ra and Amosis.

her place must be between these two princes.[1] The first series of the kings at El-Kab becomes augmented, therefore, in the second by these three new cartouches. The relationship of these kings to each other, and particularly that of the Thothmes, has been established by several other monuments, amongst which must be included the obelisks at Karnak, the long inscription in the same temple commemorative of the campaigns of Thothmes III., and some statues in the museums of London and Berlin.[2]

Third. A stela in the Gizeh Palace, dedicated to a certain Neb-ua in which Thothmes III. and Amenophis II. appear in their right order.

Fourth. An inscription at Abd-el-Gûrnah, from the tomb of that Hor-em-heb who was master of the horse under Amenophis II., Thothmes IV., and Amenophis III. So the series continues uninterruptedly, until at last we have nearly all the kings of the Eighteenth Dynasty. If we may believe Manetho and the Table of Abydos, the successor of Amenophis III. was Horus, but on studying the monuments we shall find that Horus constructed at Karnak a pylon made from the materials of a former edifice, which bore the cartouches of Khu-en-Aten (Amenophis IV.), who was therefore his

---

[1] There are two English translations of this inscription, one by S. Birch, in *Trans. Roy. Soc. of Literature*, vol. ii. p. 232; and another in *Records of the Past*, vol. iv. p. 5 *et seq.*

[2] Hatshepsu was the daughter of Thothmes I. and half sister of Thothmes II. and III., who were probably only half brothers to each other.

predecessor. That Khu-en-Aten caused the inscriptions of the reign of Amenophis III. to be erased shows that the latter king was anterior to the fanatical ruler of Tell-el-Amarna. It is impossible to doubt it ; and between Amenophis III. and Horus in the Table of Abydos must be placed him who is justly called Amenophis IV. I shall not push these details further, and show, as I might, that Amenophis IV. was not the only monarch of his race, but that he was succeeded by two or three sovereigns who, like him, were excluded from the line of legitimate kings. What I want to demonstrate is, that we can from the monuments alone reconstruct the Eighteenth Dynasty, and that we have really lost nothing by the alterations in the text of Manetho and the lacunæ in the Table of Abydos.

The monumental history of Egypt begins with the Eighteenth Dynasty. At Gebel-Barkal, close to Abû-Hammed and the Fourth Cataract, Amenophis III. built a temple that was approached by an avenue of ram-headed sphinxes. At Soleb, between the Second and Third Cataract, at Semneh just above Wady Halfah, at Amada in Nubia, are temples built by Thothmes III. One of the most beautiful edifices in Egypt, destroyed, alas ! by the vandalism of the inhabitants of Assûan, was the little temple built in the island of Elephantiné by Amenophis III.[3] A granite gateway let into the surrounding wall of Kom-Ombo calls to mind the regent

[3] The temple of Elephantiné was destroyed in 1822 by the Turkish governor of Assûan, in order to obtain stone for building a palace.

Hatshepsu. At Gebel-Silsileh are bas-reliefs relating to the campaigns of Horus ; and Thebes even now is gorgeous with the magnificent edifices of the Eighteenth Dynasty. On the left bank of the river there is Dêr-el-Bahari, and the northern part of Medinet Habû, which is the work of the Thothmes ; then there are the colossi of Amenophis III., and the magnificent hypogea of Abd-el-Gûrnah, while in the Valley of the West are three or four royal tombs of this dynasty. On the right bank there is Karnak, the greater part of which is due to Eighteenth Dynasty kings ; and Amenophis III. founded Luxor, which his successors as far as the Twenty-sixth Dynasty beautified. In other parts of Egypt are quite as many traces of these monarchs ; we shall find them at El-Kab, at Tell-el-Amarna, at Gebel-Tunah, Memphis, and Sakkarah, at the Pyramids, Heliopolis, Serbet-el-Hadim, and at Wady Magharah. In short, it is this Dynasty which has given most to the museums in Europe and Cairo. Then those splendid statues in Turin belong to the Eighteenth Dynasty ; and Cairo possesses a colossal bust of Thothmes III., which as a work of art will equa¹ them. The Gizeh Palace contains a most valuable granite stela, on which is engraven a poem composed in honour of the victories of Thothmes III. This beautiful and poetic hymn is full of inspiration, and, though many centuries older than Homer or the Bible, is one of the most valuable specimens extant of ancient literature.[4] It

---

[4] It was brought from Karnak, and there is an English version of this beautiful hymn in Brugsch-Bey's *Egypt under the Pharaohs*, new edition, p. 169 *et seq.*

was the first king of the Eighteenth Dynasty who caused those magnificent jewels to be made for the mummy of Queen Aah-hotep, the mother of Amosis, amongst the most remarkable of which are—

First. A hatchet, the ordinary symbol of divinity. The blade is of solid gold ; on one side of it are symbolic figures, on the other a representation of Amosis himself standing erect with his arms raised in the act of felling a barbarian. The handle of this axe is of wood covered with gold leaf, upon which has been carved in hieroglyphs the whole series of royal titles belonging to Amosis.

Second. An open-work pectoral of solid gold. This object is at present unique of its kind, and is shaped like an ancient Egyptian shrine. In the centre of it Amosis stands in a sacred barque, navigating himself along the waters of the celestial ocean. Two divinities, one on either side of him, pour over his head the waters of purification. The finish and execution of this rare object are wonderful. The colours are not obtained by enamelling, as is usually thought, but from small plaques of precious stones, viz., turquoise, lapis-lazuli, and red carnelian, outlined with *cloisons* of gold. On the reverse side is a series of 'point' engravings, which forms a more harmonious whole than even the principal face.

Third. A boat in solid gold mounted on a carriage with bronze wheels ; in shape it is not unlike the caïques of Constantinople or the gondolas of Venice. The oarsmen are in solid silver. In the centre of the boat stands a small person armed with a hatchet and a curved stick. Behind is the steersman, who guides the barque by means of the only helm then known—an oar with a very broad blade. In the fore part is the singer, who regulates the stroke of the oars with his voice. Close to him are engraven the cartouches of Kames. The meaning of this little boat is purely symbolic. The Egyptians thought that the soul, before arriving at its last home, must traverse the ethereal space, where it would come to fields, rivers, and canals. The barque was therefore emblematic of this journey through the other world.

Fourth. A bracelet in solid gold, with gold figures on a lapis-lazuli ground, and truly a *chef-d'œuvre* of engraving. The figures represent the divinities of the tombs.

Fifth. Three massive golden bees linked together by a golden chain. It is thought that they must have been a decoration, as the use of orders was frequent in Egypt. At El-Kab a certain Aahmes, a namesake and contemporary of the king by whose orders these jewels were made, appears to have been decorated seven times in recognition of his distinguished services, though his order is more likely to have been that of the Lion than the Bee.

Sixth. A golden diadem by which the mummy's hair was kept in place. It is ornamented with two tiny sphinxes, who are seated at either end of a sort of box shaped as a cartouche. The name of Amosis is engraved upon it in letters of gold upon a ground-work of lapis-lazuli.

Seventh. A poignard with a golden blade, and a most beautiful specimen. The hilt is inlaid with triangular designs of various colours, while the pommel is formed of four female heads charmingly executed. Down the middle of the short blade runs a band of dark-coloured metal ornamented in relief with patterns damascened in gold. On it may be read the names of Amosis accompanied on one side by a flight of grasshoppers, which gradually becomes thinner as it approaches the point of the blade, on the other by a lion who is falling upon a bull. This subject, which is entirely Asiatic in character, is all the more remarkable for being found on a monument contemporaneous with a king who during the greater part of his reign had lived in Upper Egypt.[5]

Eighth. A mirror which in shape is not unlike a palm tree. The handle is in wood picked out with gold. The disc, from which the polish has vanished, together with the thin plating of gold with which it once was covered, is made of some compound as heavy as gold, but the composition of which modern chemistry must decide.

Ninth. Two bracelets. The clasp consists of a band of gold ornamented with the cartouches of Amosis. The bracelet itself is of gold wire upon which have been strung beads of lapis-lazuli, turquoise, carnelian, and gold.

Tenth. A poignard with bronze blade. The hilt is a silver disc. In using this weapon the hilt fitted into the

[5] Is it possible that Amosis employed Asiatics (Hyksos), who were always celebrated as metal-workers?

palm of the hand, and the blade came between the first and second fingers.

Eleventh. A collar formed of innumerable small pieces, sewn on to the mummy's winding sheet, and consisting of hawks, vultures, jackals, and lions; the whole being interspersed with patterns borrowed from plant life.

Twelfth. A chain of plaited gold thread, more than a yard long, and finished by a clasp at each end in the shape of a goose's head; on this also may be read the names of Amosis. From it is suspended a scarabæus, whose legs are tucked beneath it in the most truly life-like manner. The back is of minute *cloisons* of gold encrusted with a paste of the most delicate blue. The beetle here is expressive of that creative power which endows the soul with renewed life.

Thirteenth. A bracelet, but not for the wrist. It was intended to be worn upon the upper part of the arm; upon it is represented a vulture with outstretched wings. It is a good specimen of the ordinary work of the Ancient Egyptian jewellers.

Fourteenth. A set of ten stout circlets in the form of thick rings; they were worn on the legs.

Fifteenth. A wand in black wood, ornamented with a spiral pattern in beaten gold. This wand was in Ancient Egypt a sign of power, and is carried to-day for the same purpose by the inhabitants of Nubia.[6]

[Sixty cuneiform tablets from Tell-el-Amarna, part of

[6] See Chabas, *Sur l' Usage des Bâtons de Main.*

a great 'find' in 1888. They furnish the official court correspondence of Amenophis III., and are of the greatest historical interest and importance.]

NINETEENTH DYNASTY

The names of the seven kings given by Manetho as composing this royal family have all been found on the monuments, and arranged in their right order, but the method whereby it was accomplished is too long to give here. The kings of the Nineteenth Dynasty have also left their traces—first, on monuments erected before their time, but to which they have added, and of these there are many ; and secondly, on monuments due entirely to them.

There is hardly a temple raised by the kings of the Eighteenth Dynasty upon which the monarchs of the Nineteenth have not left their mark. Especially is this the case at Thebes. The piety of Amenophis III. raised the temple at Luxor; but the two obelisks—one of which has now been transported to Paris—as well as the four colossi, in front of the principal pylon, belong to the reign of Ramses II. The pylon itself, though built by Amenophis III., is adorned with sculptures of the time of Ramses II. The same thing applies to Karnak. On the second pylon, on the splendid columns in the hypostyle hall, on the exterior of the surrounding walls, the names of Seti I. and Ramses II. alone figure. But on several occasions the latter has appropriated other people's work. On the statues and sphinxes of the Twelfth and Thirteenth Dynasties, Ramses has often erased the very cartouches which would thus have dated them, and in their place has carved his own. So carefully has this been done that the most expert archæologists have often been deceived, and have attributed monuments to the conquering king of the Nineteenth Dynasty, when in reality they were a thousand years older. Among the buildings due entirely to these three kings are, first and foremost, the tombs of Bab-el-Molûk, and particularly that of Seti I., the most magnificent subterranean construction in Egypt. Also the temple of Abû-Simbel, hollowed out of the side of a mountain, and destined to perpetuate the remembrance of the victories of Ramses II. against the Sûdanese and the Khetas. To the activity of the same king we owe the temples of Derr and Bêt-el-Walli in Nubia. Opposite to Edfû, on the caravan route from the village of Radasîeh to the gold mines of Gebel-Atoki, there is a wayside station built by Seti I. From the translation of the numerous hieroglyphs with which it is covered, we learn the reason why this monument was raised in the desert. It seems that for long the gold mines had been useless, as both men and animals perished from thirst on their way there. Seti I. therefore sank a well, in remembrance of which this temple was raised, and has remained until to-day. It is hardly necessary to say that Thebes profited largely by the munificence of the Nineteenth Dynasty kings. Within the walls of Karnak there are two or three little temples built by Ramses II.; unfortunately they are very much injured. The Ramesseum on the left bank of the river is a colossal souvenir of the same king; and to the memory of his father, Ramses I., Seti I. raised the temple of Gûrnah. The little temple of Abydos, rendered famous by the Tablet found upon its walls, is the work of Ramses II., while the great temple is due to the combined efforts of Seti I. and his son Ramses II.[7] Doubtless Memphis received some attention from the Pharaohs of this dynasty. Although rubbish heaps alone now mark the site of this illustrious city, the great portrait colossi of Ramses II. at Mitrahineh testify to the care that the king took to embellish the northern capital of Egypt. Lastly, in connection with the Nineteenth Dynasty must be mentioned the great temple of Sân, which, being very much injured, probably after the siege of that town by Amosis, was rebuilt by Ramses II., Merenptah, and Seti II.[8] From the objects found during the excavations on that ancient site, which include obelisks, monolithic granite columns, colossal stelæ, &c., we may conclude this temple to have been one of the finest raised along the Nile banks by the kings of the Nineteenth Dynasty.

Twentieth Dynasty

All the monarchs of this line called themselves Ramses in the same way that all the kings of the Thirty-

---

[7] See Mariette's *Fouilles d'Abydos.*

[8] See Tanis in *Publications of Egypt Exploration Fund.*

third Dynasty called themselves Ptolemy. We have but little more to help in the arrangement of them than a few scattered monuments, and the Theban tombs, particularly those of Bab-el-Molûk. This dynasty was too much torn by internal divisions to have time for much building. To it, however, may be attributed the magnificent pavilion and temple of Medinet-Habû and the temple of Khensu, on the southern side of Karnak, near the avenue of ram-headed sphinxes. Although this latter contains the cartouches of the Twenty-first Dynasty kings, it nevertheless was built by the later Ramessides. The fine stela brought from the temple of Khensu, and presented by M. Prisse to the National Library in Paris, also belongs to this period. From various causes it possesses great interest : on it is engraved the official statement of an event that took place in the reign of Ramses III., under the following circumstances. The king had gone into Mesopotamia to receive the tribute of the conquered country ; while there he met the daughter of one of the chieftains and married her. Some years after, Ramses being at Thebes, his father-in-law sent to him, begging for a doctor to come and cure his daughter, the sister of the queen, who had been seized with some unknown malady. A physician was despatched with the returning messenger, and found the girl was suffering from a nervous disease, which, according to the belief of those times, was occasioned by the presence within her of an evil spirit. In vain the physician tried all his healing arts ; the spirit refused to submit to

them, and the doctor at last returned to Thebes, leaving
the king's sister-in-law uncured. This happened in the
fifteenth year of Ramses' reign. Eleven years later
another envoy was sent, this time not for a physician,
but for the direct intervention of one of the Theban
gods, in the hope of bringing about the cure of the
princess. Ramses, in reply, sent the god Khensu. The
journey was a long one—it lasted a year and six months;
at the end of which time Mesopotamia was reached, and
the evil spirit, being exorcised by the Egyptian divinity,
left the princess, who immediately recovered. The stela
then goes on to relate that such miraculous cures were
wrought by the presence of the god, that the prince, at
the risk of offending his powerful ally, determined to
detain the deity in his own palace. So for nine or ten
months Khensu remained in Mesopotamia ; at the end
of which time, the prince who had ventured upon such a
daring measure had a dream wherein he saw the captive
god flying towards Egypt in the form of a golden hawk,
while he himself at the same time fell suddenly ill. This
dream was taken for an omen, whereupon the father-in-
law of Ramses promptly ordered the god to be sent
back to his own home at Thebes, which took place in
the thirty-third year of that king's reign.[9]

[9] This story has long been
known as that of 'The Possessed
Princess of Baχ-Tan.' There
is an English translation of it
in *Records of the Past*, vol. iv.
pp. 53–60. For long it was
considered authentic, but has
now been shown to be a legend
written by the Egyptian priests
for the glorification of Khensu,

THE ROYAL MUMMIES[1]

[The year 1881 was signalised by one of the most remarkable discoveries that has ever been made during the explorations in Egypt. It brought to light the mummies of no less than some thirty-eight royal personages belonging to the preceding dynasties. Ever since 1876, M. Maspero—then the Director-General of the Egyptian Explorations—had suspected that the Theban Arabs, who were ever body-snatchers, had come upon some royal tombs, which they had rifled, and whose contents they were selling to European tourists. First of all, General Campbell purchased from them for 400l. the hieratic papyrus of Pinet'em III., one of the priestly usurpers of the Twenty-first Dynasty; then M. Maspero received in the following year from M. de Saulcy some photographs of a papyrus which belonged to Queen Net'-emit, the mother of Her-Hor.[2] Afterwards, Rogers Bey showed him a tablet, then in his possession, and now in the Louvre, which M. Maspero felt sure could only belong to 'some as yet undiscovered tomb of the Her-Hor family.'

Meanwhile there appeared from time to time in Cairo funerary figures of Her-Hor himself.

and is of much later date than the period to which it purports to belong. See 'Die Bentrescht Stele,' in the *Zeitschrift*, 1883.

[1] For fuller description see *La Trouvaille de Dêr-el-Bahari*,

by G. Maspero, with photographs by H. Brugsch Bey.

[2] The papyrus is broken in two pieces; the first part of it is in the British Museum, the rest in the Louvre.

In 1881 M. Maspero went up the river, literally on
a voyage of investigation, with this much success, that
everything pointed to the fact of a certain Abd-er-Rassûl
and his brother being the possessors of the secret. So
permission for the arrest of Ahmed, the younger brother,
was obtained from the Mudîr of Keneh; but neither
bribes nor threats nor imprisonment elicited any information from him or his friends save that he was the most
truthful of Arabs, and most honest of men. After two
months of reflection in 'durance vile,' Ahmed was re-
leased, and immediately upon his return a violent quarrel
between him and his brothers broke out, with the result
that Abd-er-Rassûl the elder betook himself secretly to
Keneh, and told everything to the Mudîr, who instantly
telegraphed to the Minister of the Interior.

Within four days M. Emile Brugsch (M. Maspero
had just left for Europe) arrived, and was at once conducted to the spot at Dêr-el-Bahari which has since
become historic. There, behind a heap of rocks, was a
great hole, down which he and his companions were
lowered to a depth of thirty-six feet. On arriving at the
bottom they found themselves in a corridor, along which
they had to grope their way painfully; at a sharp turn
in it they saw carelessly thrown aside, as a thing utterly
valueless, the beautiful funeral tent of Princess Isi-em-
Kheb—a marvellous piece of leather patch-work, for
which the skins of hundreds of gazelles must have been
used. Leading out of the corridor was a chamber in
which they saw piled up in unutterable confusion some

eighteen great mummy cases, not only those of the family of the Her-Hor, but of some of the most celebrated of the Pharaohs—Thothmes III., Seti I., Ramses II. and III., &c.; while of the queens were found the coffins of Net'emit, Maat-ka-Ra, and Isi-em-Kheb. With all the speed possible, the contents of both chambers and corridor were removed to Bûlaq : these consisted of mummies, coffins, funerary furniture, statuettes, alabaster canopic vases, and terra-cotta jars, etc.

In 1886, M. Maspero unrolled some of these royal mummies, and in the Gizeh Palace the traveller may stand face to face with Sekenen-Ra, on whose forehead may be clearly seen the grim death wound which felled him while fighting for his country against the Hyksos ; the small form, barely over five feet, of Thothmes III., the great warrior-king ; the calm, placid face of Seti I., the art-loving builder-king of Abydos fame ; and the harsh features of Ramses II., who withstood Moses. How came all these kings and queens to have been thus torn from their own tombs in the valleys close by, and huddled together in this almost inaccessible chamber ? The 'Amherst' and 'Abbott' Papyri give us the clue, and from them we learn that in the Twentieth Dynasty it was found that the tombs of Sebek-em-Saf and his queen Nub-khas had been violated ; in consequence of which periodical inspections of both the royal mummies and their resting-places were instituted—the inspectors being obliged to record their visit upon the winding-sheet of the deceased as well as on the coffin. In the troublous

times that followed, the bodies of many of the royalties
were removed for greater safety, and in this weird hiding-
place were stowed away the mummies of the greatest of
Egypt's kings, together with those of the Her-Hor family,
in the hope of successfully baffling the cupidity of the
grave-hunters.

In 1891 a large collection of mummies—supposed to
be those of the high priests of Amen—and a considerable
number of papyri were discovered in a secluded spot
near Queen Hatshepsu's temple.   They are at the Gizeh
Palace awaiting scientific examination.—ED.]

TWENTY-FIRST DYNASTY

On the temple situated between Karnak and Luxor
are the cartouches of the high priests who completed it ;
while the monuments of the legitimate dynasty will be
found chiefly at Sân.   Some of the cartouches of this
line have been preserved on some architraves, and some
gold plates which are now in the Gizeh Palace.

TWENTY-SECOND DYNASTY

Of this family, which came originally from Tell Basta,
Manetho gives ten names, while its genealogy is attested
by some inscriptions on a statue of the Nile god belonging to the British Museum ; by a long legend which
covers one of the external walls of Karnak ; and by some
invaluable texts found some years ago in the Apis tombs

of Sakkarah and now in the Louvre. For the rest we do not know of any important building erected by these kings ; though it is possible that persevering excavations at Tell Basta may bring to light some traces of the monuments with which the Twenty-second Dynasty adorned their capital.[3]

TWENTY-THIRD DYNASTY

This was a period of trouble in Egyptian history, and our knowledge of it rests chiefly upon a granite stela found at Gebel-Barkal. It is a remarkable fact that this monument is Cushite, and not Egyptian. These Cushites, when becoming a separate kingdom, adopted the religion, writing, and language of the Egyptians ; their civilization was, therefore, so to speak, the daughter of Egyptian civilization. The stela also shows that the Ethiopians subdued Egypt, and it is clear from it that they imposed their yoke upon the mother country. The Twenty-third Dynasty was an unhappy epoch ; for Egypt was divided between several collateral families, out of all of which Manetho gives but three kings (who came originally from Sân) as legitimate. The Apis stelæ, however, show another line, reigning at Memphis, and, like that of Sân, composed of three kings, and from the stela at Gebel-Barkal we find several provinces of Egypt obeying territorial kings, who are certainly neither those of Manetho nor yet of the Apis tombs.

[3] See ' Bubastis,' vol. viii. *Egypt Exploration Fund.*

TWENTY-FOURTH DYNASTY

This dynasty possesses, according to Manetho, but one king, whose Egyptian name was for long unknown. Now, at last, the stones of the Serapēum have revealed it—Bocchoris ; and, so far as we know at present, they are the only records of his reign. There is nothing to prove that the Ethiopians were not already in possession of Southern Egypt.

TWENTY-FIFTH DYNASTY

We now come to the Cushite supremacy in Egypt, and must not be surprised, therefore, to find the names of the sovereigns of this dynasty in the Sûdan as well as in Egypt. Manetho gives three kings ; and evidently this is from the point of view of the Egyptians. According to the Apis stelæ, Taharaqa, the third monarch of this line, was succeeded by Psammetichus, the first king of the Twenty-sixth Dynasty. Now, if the Ethiopians (like the Egyptians) had left historical records, we should have one more name, that of the husband of Queen Ameniritis, whose statue is in the Gizeh Palace. This king, Piankhi, succeeded Taharaqa, and ruled over Upper Egypt, while the twelve confederate princes governed the other portions of the kingdom. When Psammetichus ascended the throne, fifteen years after the fall of Taharaqa, he paid no heed to the claims of the allies, but considered himself as having been sovereign of the country from the day that the third Ethiopian king ceased to reign.[4]

TWENTY-SIXTH DYNASTY

With the accession of this dynasty, comes the time when the Greeks were allowed freer access to Egypt, and when the Nile country begins to be frequently mentioned in their writings. Classical tradition gives a fairly exact list of the kings of this Twenty-sixth Dynasty, and it can be studied also from Manetho ; while the Apis stelæ form an imposing collection of monuments contemporaneous with Psammetichus and his successors. Foremost in importance are the official epitaphs of the Apis bulls ; they are all arranged on a uniform model ; they give the date of the bull's birth, and that of his death, the length of his life in years, months, and days ; the whole, in accordance with the Egyptian mode, being reckoned by the year of the reigning monarch.

Every one can see the value of such records. Suppose, for instance, that one of these tablets stated that a certain Apis bull was born in the fifty-third year of a particular king's reign, and that he died in the sixteenth year of another's reign, at the age of seventeen years ; we should at once recognise that the two kings must have followed one another chronologically, and that

[4] For more information concerning Taharaqa, the Tirhaka of 2 Kings xix. 9 and Isaiah xxxvii. 9, and the Tirquu of Assyrian records, see *Mémoire* *sur les rapports de l'Égypte et de l'Assyrie dans l'antiquité éclaircis par l'étude des Textes Cunéiformes*, by Jules Oppert.

the first king must have reigned fifty-four years and the second sixteen at the least. Apply this method to all the kings of the Twenty-sixth Dynasty, and the Apis tombs will give not only the sequence of the kings, but the length in years of the whole of this royal family. Apart from the Serapēum, the monuments of the dynasty are rare ; though the tombs of the Assassif at Thebes, which are celebrated for the breadth and finish of their bas-reliefs, date from this period.

On the rocks at Assûan and Hammamât, at Thebes, Abydos, and Sakkarah are to be found here and there a few souvenirs of those princes who occupied at this date the throne of Egypt. It is not that the Twenty-sixth Dynasty was less given than the others to leaving remembrances of itself behind; but rather that at the moment of its existence the tide of civilization was flowing towards the north, and that all the country's forces were being centred at Saïs, the capital of the Twenty-sixth Dynasty ; which, according to Herodotus, was one of the most flourishing towns in the kingdom. Here Apries built a temple which was second to none in Egypt ; and here, too, Amasis raised that huge portico which, from its dimensions and the size and quality of its stone, surpassed every other monument of the kind. To this prince also are due colossal statues, and sphinxes of enormous proportions ; also a colossus 75 feet high, a companion to the one erected at Memphis by Amasis. This king did not limit himself to the construction of porticoes only, but caused enormous blocks to be con-

veyed to Saïs for the restoration of the temple ; some or
which were quarried at Tûrah, while others and larger came
from Assûan.   But more wonderful still was the monolithic chapel in the temple at Saïs made from the stone
of Elephantiné.   Two thousand boatmen were occupied
for three months in conveying it there.   Its external
measurements were 39 ft. long, 22 ft. wide, and 12 ft.
high ; and after the interior had been hollowed out, this
gigantic mass weighed over 428 tons.   Herodotus leaves
us no doubts as to the magnificence of the Saïte kings
town, and it is evident that they did for it what ten
centuries before the monarchs of the Eighteenth and
Nineteenth Dynasties had done for Thebes.   Unfortunately, Saïs has disappeared for ever, and a confused
heap of ruins is all that is left of a town that was once
the home of civilization and art ! [5]   One hardly dares to

[5] Herodotus says : ' This prince erected at Saïs, in honour of Minerva, a magnificent portico, exceeding everything of the kind in size and grandeur. The stones of which it was composed were of a very uncommon size and quality, and decorated with a number of colossal statues and andro-sphinxes of enormous magnitude. To repair this temple he also collected stones of amazing thickness, part of which he brought from the quarries of Memphis and part from the city of Elephantiné, which is distant from Saïs a journey of about twenty days. But what in my opinion is most of all to be admired is an edifice which he brought from Elephantiné constructed of one entire stone. The carriage of it employed 2,000 men, all of whom were pilots, for an entire period of three years. . . It is placed at the entrance of the temple. The reason it was carried no further is this : the architect, reflecting on his long and continued fatigue, sighed deeply, which incident Amasis

hope even that excavations made on the site of it might bring to light a few vestiges of the brilliant Twenty-sixth Dynasty.

TWENTY-SEVENTH DYNASTY

The Persians now are in possession of the banks of the Nile ; and Cambyses, humiliated by three defeats, treated Egypt as a conquered country; while it was with the utmost repugnance that Egypt submitted to the foreign yoke ; consequently there were perpetual revolts through-out the land, resulting in an absence of monuments. The name of Cambyses may, however, be read on some of the Apis stelæ. Darius, too, has left traces of his presence in the country at Hammamât, and in the oasis of Khargeh, where he built a temple to Amen. In many inscriptions the name of Artaxerxes appears, and it may also be read upon two vases, one in the National Library in Paris, the other in the treasury of St. Mark's, at Venice. Besides these few specimens the only monument of the Persian domination in Egypt is the ruin brought about by the fury of Cambyses. It is to Manetho that we owe the list of these kings.

construed as an omen, and obliged him to desist. Some, however, affirm that one of those employed to move it by levers was crushed by it, for which reason it was advanced no further.'

TWENTY-EIGHTH, TWENTY-NINTH, AND THIRTIETH DYNASTIES

Although Egypt was again her own mistress, she was nevertheless constantly in trouble, and the enemy was never far from her gates. Still for all this, there are some monuments of these dynasties left, which are worthy of a more flourishing epoch. Nectanebo II. began the grand temple at Philæ, and Medinet Habû and Karnak were added to by Nectanebo I. This prince also completed the Serapēum at Memphis, and erected a fine pylon at the entrance of these subterranean tombs. Acoris and Nepheritis also embellished the temples with statues and bas-reliefs. Those magnificent granite sarcophagi in the Louvre, the Berlin Museum, and the Gizeh Palace are of this period ;[6] while the sarcophagus of Nectanebo was removed from Alexandria for transport to London. It is curious to notice that, although these dynasties declined in political importance, there are as yet no signs visible of that rapid decadence in Egyptian Art which took place within a few years of the Greek occupation of Egypt.

THIRTY-FIRST DYNASTY

The Persians are again masters of Egypt, but Manetho is the only person who takes any notice of this second Persian Dynasty. From the Egyptian monuments

[6] The British Museum also contains a fine specimen.

we can hardly find even the names of those kings who formed the Thirty-first Dynasty.

THIRTY-SECOND DYNASTY

A Macedonian Dynasty, whose head and chief was Alexander the Great.

Manetho's lists here come to an end, and the only means by which we can arrange the kings of this period chronologically are the monumental records illustrated and completed by the narratives of the classical writers. In the island of Elephantiné the name of Alexander I. may be read on the two jambs of a granite doorway ; while at Karnak, Philip Arrhidœus, his brother, constructed the beautiful granite chamber in the midst of the temple of Thothmes III., which occupies the principal place in front of the sanctuary. Alexander II. also figures in the bas-reliefs on the walls of the temples of Karnak and Luxor as the legitimate king of Egypt.

THIRTY-THIRD DYNASTY

Since the Nineteenth Dynasty no royal family has raised so many buildings in Egypt as did the Thirty-third Dynasty. Not only did the Ptolemies restore and complete the old sanctuaries, but they also erected many new temples. In Nubia there are those of Dakkeh and Kalabsheh ; while they have made the lovely little island of Philæ one of the most beautiful sites in the world. In

Egypt the temple of Kom-Ombo, notwithstanding that it is spoilt by the bad taste of the period, is a model of powerful architecture. Esneh, though less debased, is ruined by being partly buried beneath the modern town. Erment has now entirely disappeared. But while decorating Alexandria with splendid edifices of which we can no longer judge, the Ptolemies did not forget Thebes. On the left bank of the river are Dêr-el-Medineh and the little temple on Birket Habû ; while on the right are the large isolated gateway to the north of the temple of Karnak, and the similar one through which one passes on the way from Luxor to the temple of Khensu ; and also a small building by the side of this temple. And what of the incomparable temple of Denderah, built in honour of Cæsarion and dedicated to the gods of the country, and above all Edfû? There indeed is a perfect treasury of texts—hundreds of yards in length—the deciphering of which will likely enough prove to be the resuscitation of the mythology and geography of Egypt, as it was in the days of the Ptolemies. Lastly I must mention that at El-Kab, Motana, Ekmîm, Behbit,[7] as well as in many other places, the names of the Ptolemies may be found. To them also belongs the finest part of the Serapēum of Sakkarah, as well as the gigantic sarcophagi that were found in it. In enumerating the monuments of this period we must not omit that celebrated fragment known as the Rosetta Stone. It was discovered some years ago by French soldiers who were digging an entrenchment near the

[7] Near Mahallet-el-Kebîr.

redoubts at Rosetta, and has proved of the greatest importance in the study of Egyptology.   Upon it are engraven
three inscriptions, two of which are in the Egyptian
language, and are written in the script of that particular
time.   One of them is in the hieroglyphic characters
which was the form of writing used by the priests, and,
though only fourteen lines long, is imperfect owing to the
fracture of the stone ; the other is in the cursive characters
in vogue amongst the common people, and of this there
are thirty-two lines.   The third inscription is fifty-four
lines in length, and is in Greek ; and it is in this last that
lies the interest of the Rosetta monument.   From the
interpretation of the Greek text we find that it is a version
of the two Egyptian inscriptions above it, so that on the
Rosetta Stone we have a translation, in a well-known
tongue (Greek), of a text which at the time of its discovery
was inscribed in a lost language.   To proceed from the
known to the unknown is ever a legitimate operation, and
the value of the Rosetta Stone is that it furnished, by
these means, the key to the mysterious writing of which
Egypt so long guarded the secret.   However, it must not
be thought that the deciphering of the hieroglyphs by
means of the Rosetta Stone was arrived at all at once, or
without tentative methods.   On the contrary, scholars
were occupied in working at it with but little success for
twenty years, until at last Champollion appeared.   Until
his day it was always thought that every hieroglyph was
a symbol ; that is to say, that each character contained
in itself a complete idea.   Champollion, however, dis-

covered that in the Egyptian writing there were signs conveying definite sounds—that it was in fact alphabetic. For instance, he noticed that wherever the name of Ptolemy occurred in the Greek text of the Rosetta Stone, in about the corresponding place in the Egyptian writing was a small elliptic frame containing a number of signs. He therefore concluded, first of all, that in the hieroglyphic system attention was called to the names of the kings by enclosing them within a shield, to which he gave the name of cartouche ; secondly, that the signs contained in this cartouche must be letter for letter the word Ptolemy.[8] Supposing, then, the vowels to be omitted, he was in possession of five letters, P, T, L, M, S. Now Champollion knew already by a Greek inscription engraven upon the obelisk at Philæ that the hieroglyphic cartouche upon it ought to be that of Cleopatra. If, then, his first reading was correct, the P, T, and L of Ptolemy should be found again in this second proper name with K and R in addition. Thus these two names, Ptolemy and Cleopatra, were the foundation of his alphabet, until, little by little, he acquired nearly all the consonants. He was then practically in possession of the Egyptian alphabet. But the language had still to be interpreted. To pronounce words is idle unless the meaning of them is comprehensible. And here the genius of Champollion displayed itself fully : he discovered that his alphabet derived from these two proper names, and applied to other words in the language, produced words in Coptic,

[8] The omission of the vowels is frequent in Eastern languages.

which, though not so much studied as Greek, had for a long time been an accessible language. This time he had indeed discovered the secret. The Ancient Egyptian language was nothing but Coptic written in hieroglyphs, or rather Coptic was but the language of the Pharaohs transcribed in Greek characters. The rest came rapidly enough. Champollion went on gradually proceeding from the known to the unknown, until at last he was able to lay the foundation of that noble science which has for its object the deciphering of hieroglyphic texts. Such is the history of the Rosetta Stone. Owing to its discovery the Egyptian monuments are no longer objects of hopeless curiosity, and Ancient Egypt has again been restored to her own place in the story of the nations. Soon after the discovery of the monument it was taken to Alexandria, where it fell into the hands of the English, who on leaving Egypt took it, along with several other monuments once belonging to the French army, to London, and deposited it in the British Museum.

THIRTY-FOURTH DYNASTY

After lasting for 5400 years, the Empire of Mena fell, and from henceforth Egypt was but a province of the Roman Empire. The prefects erected several monuments at Alexandria, amongst which are Pompey's Pillar, Hadrian's town of Antinoë (Shêkh-Abadeh), and the tomb, well worthy of the ancient kings, that he erected to the memory of his favourite Antinoüs. In front of it

were sphinxes and obelisks ; one of which latter monuments is in Rome, where it is called the Barberini obelisk.
At Kalabsheh, Dendûr, Dakkeh, Philæ, Edfû, Esneh,
Erment, and Denderah, the Roman emperors continued
the work of the Ptolemies. But symptoms of decadence
were already visible in the apparent prosperity. The art
of Khufu, the Usertsens, Thothmes, Ramessides, and
Psammetichus degenerated daily ; the manners, language,
and writing were modified ; and Egypt began to totter
until under Theodosius she fell.

We shall feel that our self-imposed task in the Appendix has been thoroughly completed if the reader be persuaded by it of this one fact only—that the history of
Ancient Egypt, long, interesting, and chequered as it was,
is truly worthy of the title of history, and that the strongest
proofs of this fact lie in the country's own monuments.

THE DYNASTIES AND PRINCIPAL KINGS
OF ANCIENT EGYPT

ANCIENT EMPIRE

DYNASTIES		DURATION
I–II.	Thinite	555 Years
III–V.	Memphite	746 ,,
VI.	Elephantiné	203 ,,
VII–VIII.	Memphite	{ 142 ,,
		70 Days
IX–X.	Heracleopolite	294 Years

MIDDLE EMPIRE

XI–XIII.	Theban	666 ,,
XIV.	Xoïte	184 ,,
XV–XVII.	Hyksos (Delta)	511 ,,

NEW EMPIRE

XVIII–XX.	Theban	593 ,,
XXI.	Tanite	130 ,,
XXII.	Bubastite	170 ,,
XXIII.	Tanite	89 ,,
XXIV.	Saïte	6 ,,
XXV.	Ethiopian	50 ,,
XXVI.	Saïte	138 ,,
XXVII.	Persian	121 ,,
XXVIII.	Saïte	7 ,,
XXIX.	Mendesian	21 ,,
XXX.	Sebennyte	38 ,,
XXXI.	Persian	8 ,,

PRINCIPAL KINGS

	DYNASTIES
Mena ⎫ Teta ⎬ Hesepti ⎭	I.
Ba-en-neter	II.
Sneferu	III.
Khufu ⎫ Khafra ⎬ Menkau-Ra ⎭	IV.
Unas	V.
Teta ⎫ Pepi I. ⎪ Pepi II. ⎬ Queen Nitocris ⎭	VI.
Amen-em-hat I. ⎫ Usertsen I. ⎪ Amen-em-hat II. ⎪ Usertsen II. ⎬ Usertsen III. ⎪ Amen-em-hat III. ⎪ Amen-em-hat IV. ⎭	XII.
Sekenen-Ra	XVII.
Aahmes I. ⎫ Amen-hotep I. ⎪ Thothmes I. ⎪ Thothmes II. ⎪ Queen Hatshepsu ⎪ Thothmes III. ⎬ Amen-hotep II. ⎪ Thothmes IV. ⎪ Amen-hotep III. ⎪ Amen-hotep IV. ⎪ (Khu-en-Aten) ⎭	XVIII.
Seti I. ⎫ Ramses II. ⎬ Merenptah ⎭	XIX.

DYNASTIES

Ramses III.	XX.
Her-Hor	XXI.
Shashanq I. (Shishak) ⎱ Osorkon II. (Zerah ?) ⎰	XXII.
Tefnekht. (Piankhi King of Ethiopia took Memphis)	XXIII.
Bakenranef (Bocchoris)	XXIV.

Shabaka. His sister Amen-
  iritis married Piankhi II.
  and their daughter became
  the queen of Psamethek I.
Shabataka.
Taharaqa (Tirhakah)
	XXV.

Psamethek I. Neku II. (Necho) . . . . . Uahabra (Hophra)	XXVI.
Nekthorheb (Nectanebo I.) ⎱ Nektnebef (,, II.) ⎰	XXX.

BOOKS OF REFERENCE

The History of Herodotus, Book ii.
Strabo, Book xvii.
Diodorus, Book i.
Unger's Manetho.
De Iside et Osiride. Plutarch.
Egypt under the Pharaohs. H. Brugsch.
Gli Hyksos. De Cara.
Histoire des Peuples de l'Orient. Maspero.
Mélanges Égyptologiques. Chabas.
Contes Populaires. Maspero.
Monuments of Upper Egypt. Mariette.
Aegypten und die Bücher Moses. Ebers.
The Fleet of an Egyptian Queen. Dümichen.
Manners and Customs of the Ancient Egyptians. Gardiner
    Wilkinson.
Les Monuments de l'Art Antique. Rayet.
The Art of Ancient Egypt. Perrot and Chipiez.
Egyptian Archæology. Maspero.
Une Enquête Judiciaire à Thèbes. Maspero.
The Hibbert Lectures for 1879. P. le Page Renouf.
Égypte à Petites Journées. A. Rhoné.
Fouilles d'Abydos. Mariette.
Études Égyptiennes. Maspero.
L'Art Égyptien. Prisse.
La Trouvaille de Dér-el-Bahari. Maspero and Brugsch.
The Fayûm and Lake Mœris. Major Brown, R.E.
Relation de l'Égypte. Abd el-Latif.
The Publications of the Egypt Exploration Fund.
Egypt's Place in Universal History. Bunsen.
Cities of Egypt. R. S. Poole.
Dictionnaire d'Archéologie Égyptienne. P. Pierret.
Voyage de la Haute-Égypte. C. Blanc.
The Monumental History of Egypt. Osburn.
I Monumenti, &c. Rosellini.
Revue de l'Histoire de Religion. Maspero.
La Sculpture Égyptienne. Soldi.
La Bible et les Découvertes Modernes. Vigouroux.
Aegypten und Aegyptisches Leben im Alterthum. Erman.
Denkmäler aus Aegypten. Lepsius.
The Tell-el Amarna Tablets. Budge and Bezold.

TABLE OF THE ANCIENT EGYPTIAN CALENDAR IN ITS NORMAL FORM, COMPARED WITH THE EGYPTIAN YEAR

Sacred Sothic Year			Alexandrian Year		Julian Year		Ancient Egyptian Seasons
Day	Month	Day	Day	Month	Day	Month	
1	Thoth (I.)	1	26	Epiphi	20	July	
6	"	6	1	Mesori (XII.)	25	"	
31	Paophi (II.)	1	26	"	19	August	
36	"	6	1	"	24	"	
—		—	—	Intercalary Days	—		
40	"	10	5	Thoth (I.)	28	"	
41	Athyr (III.)	11	1	"	29	"	
61	"	1	21	"	18	September	I.
71	"	11	1	Paophi (II.)	28	"	The Inundation
91	Khoiak IV.	1	21	"	18	October	
110	"	11	1	Athyr III.	28	"	

							Season
121	1	Tybi (V.)	21	Khoiakh (IV.)	17	November	
131	11	„	1	„	27	„	
151	1	Mekhir (VI.)	21	„	17	December	II. The Winter
161	11	„	1	Tybi (V.)	27	„	
181	1	Phamenoth (VII.)	21	„	16	January	
191	11	„	1	Mekhir (VI.)	26	„	
211	1	Pharmuthi (VIII.)	21	„	15	February	
221	11	„	1	Phamenoth (VII.)	25	„	
241	1	Pakhons (IX.)	21	„	17	March	
251	11	„	1	Pharmuthi (VIII.)	27	„	
271	1	Panoi (X.) (Payni)	21	„	16	April	
281	11	„	1	Pakhons (IX.)	26	„	III. The Summer
301	1	Epiphi (XI.)	21	„	16	May	
311	11	„	1	Payni (X.)	26	„	
331	1	Mesori (XII.)	21	„	15	June	
341	11	„	1	Epiphi (XI.)	25	„	
361	1	Intercalary Days	21	„	15	July	
365	5		25		19	„	

L 2

INDEX

PRINTED BY
SPOTTISWOODE AND CO., NEW-STREET SQUARE
LONDON

MURRAY'S FOREIGN HANDBOOKS

WITH MAPS AND PLANS.

'Mr. MURRAY has succeeded in identifying his countrymen all the world over. Into every nook which an Englishman can penetrate he carries his **RED HANDBOOK.** He trusts to his **MURRAY** because it is thoroughly English and reliable.'—TIMES.

HANDBOOK—EGYPT : THE NILE, THROUGH EGYPT, NUBIA, ALEXANDRIA, CAIRO, THE PYRAMIDS, THEBES, THE SUEZ CANAL, PENINSULA OF SINAI, THE OASES, THE FYOOM, &c. 15s. 1891.

HANDBOOK — THE RIVIERA &c.: PROVENCE, DAUPHINÉ, THE ALPES MARITIMES, AVIGNON, NÎMES, ARLES, MARSEILLES, NICE, CANNES, MONACO, MENTONE, BORDIGHERA, SAN REMO. New Edition. 1892.

HANDBOOK—MEDITERRANEAN ISLANDS: The COASTS OF AFRICA, SPAIN, ITALY, DALMATIA, GREECE, ASIA MINOR, CORSICA, SARDINIA, SICILY, MALTA, THE BALEARIC ISLANDS, CRETE, RHODES, CYPRUS, &c. In Two Parts. 21s. 1892.

HANDBOOK—ALGERIA AND TUNIS: ALGIERS, CONSTANTINE, ORAN, THE ATLAS RANGE, &c. 12s. 1890.

HANDBOOK—NORTH ITALY AND VENICE: TURIN, MILAN, PAVIA, CREMONA, THE ITALIAN LAKES, BERGAMO, BRESCIA, VERONA, MANTUA, VICENZA, PADUA, VENICE, FERRARA, BOLOGNA, RAVENNA, RIMINI, PARMA, MODENA, PLACENZA, GENOA, &c. 10s. 1891.

HANDBOOK — CENTRAL ITALY AND FLORENCE : LUCCA, TUSCANY, UMBRIA, THE MARCHES, AND THE LATE PATRIMONY OF ST. PETER. In Two Parts. 10s. 1892.

HANDBOOK—ROME AND ITS ENVIRONS. 10s. 1888.

HANDBOOK—SOUTH ITALY AND SICILY: NAPLES, POMPEII, HERCULANEUM, VESUVIUS ; SORRENTO ; CAPRI, &c. : AMALFI, PÆSTUM, POZZUOLI, CAPUA, TARANTO, BARI ; BRINDISI, ROME TO NAPLES, PALERMO, MESSINA, SYRACUSE, CATANIA. In Two Parts. 12s. 1892.

HANDBOOK—HOLY LAND): SYRIA, PALESTINE, SINAI, EDOM, JERUSALEM, PETRA, DAMASCUS, AND PALMYRA. 18s. 1892.

JOHN MURRAY, Albemarle Street

MURRAY'S HANDBOOKS

THOROUGHLY REVISED ON A NEW SYSTEM.

To meet the requirements of modern travel, consequent upon the great extension of railway systems throughout Europe and elsewhere, Mr. Murray has, during the past few years, *reorganised* and in a great measure *reconstructed* and *re-written* his Handbooks. In the words of the SATURDAY REVIEW, 'The whole series has been in process of being gradually "put through the mill" in regard of all modern requirements, while it still retains the characteristic (in which no modern series has yet even attempted to touch it) of being thoroughly scholarly.'

The arrangement of the main routes, by being made to coincide as nearly as possible with those of the official Railway Time-tables, has secured the utmost simplicity of plan with the greatest facility of reference.

The historical and other information, not found in every Guide, yet always considered of value and interest to the most intelligent travellers, has been retained, whilst the practical information has been made as detailed and accurate as is compatible with the nature and limits of a traveller's guide.

A special feature in the recent editions of the Handbook is the INDEX AND DIRECTORY, where all information that is liable to change, relating to

HOTELS,	DOCTORS,
RESTAURANTS,	BANKS,
CAFÉS,	SHOPS,
CHURCH SERVICES,	STEAMBOATS, &c.

will be found in a compact and convenient form at the end of the books, where it is frequently reprinted and brought up to date.

In issuing these new editions Mr. Murray is virtually publishing a *Series of new Handbooks*, which, with a largely *increased number of maps and plans*, are calculated to meet all the present requirements of travellers.

THE FOLLOWING HANDBOOKS HAVE BEEN RECONSTRUCTED ON THE NEW SYSTEM.

Maps and Plans.

SWITZERLAND. Edited by W. A. B. COOLIDGE, M.A.   22

NORTH ITALY ⎫
                   ⎰ Edited by II. W. PULLEN, M.A.,   34
CENTRAL ,,   ⎱ Author of 'Dame Europa's School'   24
SOUTH ,,   ⎭   20

,, GERMANY 34

BELGIUM AND HOLLAND 18

FRANCE. PART I. 36

,, PART II. 23

SPAIN 43

MEDITERRANEAN ⎫ Edited by Sir LAMBERT ⎰ 80
ALGERIA AND TUNIS ⎭ PLAYFAIR, K.C.M.G. ⎱ 12

INDIA AND CEYLON 55

*SYRIA AND PALESTINE. Edited by HASKETT SMITH, M.A. 29

*EGYPT 34

' No one can read the very full introduction to the new edition of Murray's " Handbook to Lower and Upper Egypt" without longing to taste of the various joys therein described. Altogether the general information covers a hundred pages, and a careful study of this introduction will not only put the intending visitor in possession of all he wants to know concerning modes of travelling, hotels, money, servants, &c., but will give him such a knowledge of the climate, the geography, the history, the people, and the archæology of Egypt, as will enable him to do his sightseeing with intelligence.'—TIMES.

* Owing to the peculiar nature of this country it has been found impossible to carry out the new system in its entirety, but the book is none the less most thoroughly revised and brought up to date.

JOHN MURRAY, Albemarle Street.

ALBEMARLE STREET, LONDON,
July, 1892.

MR. MURRAY'S
GENERAL LIST OF WORKS.

ALBERT MEMORIAL. A Descriptive and Illustrated Account of the National Monument at Kensington. Illustrated by numerous Engravings. By DOYNE C. BELL. With 24 Plates. Folio. 12*l.* 12*s.*
———— HANDBOOK. 16mo. 1*s.*; Illustrated, 2*s.* 6*d.*

ABBOTT (REV. J.). Memoirs of a Church of England Missionary in the North American Colonies. Post 8vo. 2*s.*

ABERCROMBIE (JOHN). Enquiries concerning the Intellectual Powers and the Investigation of Truth. Fcap. 8vo. 3*s.* 6*d.*

ACLAND (REV. C.). Manners and Customs of India. Post 8vo. 2*s.*

ACWORTH (W. M.) The Railways of England. With 56 Illustrations. 8vo. 14*s.*
———— The Railways of Scotland. Map. Crown 8vo. 5*s.*
———— The Railways and the Traders. The Railway Rates Question in Theory and Practice. Crown 8vo. 6*s.*, or Popular Edit. 1*s.*

ÆSOP'S FABLES. A New Version. By REV. THOMAS JAMES. With 100 Woodcuts, by TENNIEL and WOLFE. Post 8vo. 2*s.* 6*d.*

AGRICULTURAL (ROYAL) JOURNAL.

AINGER (A. C.). Latin Grammar. [See ETON.]
———— An English-Lat'n Gradus, or Verse Dictionary. On a New Plan, with carefully Selected Epithets and Synonyms. Intended to Simplify the Composition of Latin Verses. Crown 8vo. (450 pp.) 9*s.*

ALICE (PRINCESS); GRAND DUCHESS OF HESSE. Letters to H.M. THE QUEEN. With a Memoir by H.R.H. Princess Christian. Portrait. Crown 8vo. 7*s.* 6*d.*, or Original Edition, 12*s.*

AMBER-WITCH (THE). A most interesting Trial for Witchcraft. Translated by LADY DUFF GORDON. Post 8vo. 2*s.*

AMERICA (THE RAILWAYS OF). Their Construction, Development, Management, and Appliances. By Various Writers. With an Introduction by T. M. COOLEY. With 200 Illustrations. Large 8vo. 31*s.* 6*d.*
———— [See BATES, NADAILLAC, RUMBOLD.]

APOCRYPHA: With a Commentary Explanatory and Critical. By Dr. Salmon, Prof. Fuller, Archdeacon Farrar, Archdeacon Gifford, Canon Rawlinson, Dr. Edersheim, Rev. J. H. Lupton, Rev. C. J. Ball. Edited by HENRY WACE, D.D. 2 vols. Medium 8vo. 50*s.*

ARCHITECTURE: A Profession or an Art. Thirteen short Essays on the qualifications and training of Architects. Edited by R. NORMAN SHAW, R.A. and T. G. JACKSON, A.R.A. 8vo.

ARGYLL (DUKE OF). Unity of Nature. 8vo. 12*s.*
———— Reign of Law. Crown 8vo. 5*s.*
———— Neglected Elements in Economic Science. 8vo.

ARISTOTLE. [See GROTE.]

ARTHUR'S (LITTLE) History of England. By LADY CALLCOTT. New Edition, continued to 1878. With Woodcuts. Fcap. 8vo. 1*s.* 6*d.*
———— HISTORY OF FRANCE, from the Earliest Times to the Fall of the Second Empire. With Woodcuts. Fcap. 8vo. 2*s.* 6*d.*

AUSTIN (JOHN). GENERAL JURISPRUDENCE; or, The Philosophy of Positive Law. Edited by ROBERT CAMPBELL. 2 Vols. 8vo. 32*s.*

B

AUSTIN (JOHN). STUDENT'S EDITION, compiled from the above
work, by ROBERT CAMPBELL. Post 8vo. 12s.
———— Analysis of. By GORDON CAMPBELL. Post 8vo. 6s.

AUSTRALIA. [See LUMHOLTZ.]

BABER (E. C.). Travels in W. China. Maps. Royal 8vo. 5s.

BAINES (THOMAS). Greenhouse and Stove Plants, Flower-
ing and Fine-Leaved. Palms, Ferns, and Lycopodiums. With full
details of the Propagation and Cultivation. 8vo. 8s. 6d.

BALDWIN BROWN (PROF G.). The Fine Arts. With Illustrations. Crown 8vo. 3s. 6d. (University Extension Series.)

BARKLEY (H. C.). Five Years among the Bulgarians and Turks
between the Danube and the Black Sea. Post 8vo. 10s. 6d.
———— Bulgaria Before the War. Post 8vo. 10s. 6d.
———— My Boyhood. Woodcuts. Post 8vo. 6s.
———— Studies in the Art of Rat-catching. Post 8vo.
3s. 6d.
———— Ride through Asia Minor and Armenia. With
Sketches of the Character, Manners, and Customs of both the Mussul-
man and Christian Inhabitants. Crown 8vo. 10s. 6d.

BARROW (JOHN). Life of Sir Francis Drake. Post 8vo. 2s.

BATES (H. W.). Records of a Naturalist on the Amazons during
Eleven Years' Adventure and Travel. Illustrations. Post 8vo. 7s. 6d.

BATTLE ABBEY ROLL. [See CLEVELAND.]

BEACONSFIELD'S (LORD) Letters, and " Correspondence with
his Sister," 1830—1852. Portrait. Crown 8vo. 2s.

BEATRICE, H.R.H. PRINCESS. Adventures in the Life of Count
George Albert of Erbach. A True Story. Translated from the German.
Portraits and Woodcuts. Crown 8vo. 10s. 6d.

BECKETT (SIR EDMUND), (LORD GRIMTHORPE). "Should the
Revised New Testament be Authorised?" Post 8vo. 6s.

BELL (DOYNE C.). Notices of the Historic Persons buried in
the Chapel of the Tower of London. Illustrations. Crown 8vo. 14s.

BENJAMIN'S Persia & the Persians. Illustrations. 8vo. 24s.

BENSON (ARCHBISHOP). The Cathedral; its necessary place in
the Life and Work of the Church. Post 8vo. 6s.

BERKELEY (HASTINGS). Wealth and Welfare: Crown 8vo. 6s.
———— Japanese Letters; Eastern Impressions of
Western Men and Manners, as contained in the Correspondence of
Tokiwara and Yashiri. Post 8vo. 6s.

BERTHELOT ON EXPLOSIVES. [See CUNDILL.]

BERTRAM (JAS. G.). Harvest of the Sea: an Account of British
Food Fishes, Fisheries and Fisher Folk. Illustrations. Post 8vo. 9s.

BIBLE COMMENTARY. EXPLANATORY AND CRITICAL. With
a REVISION of the TRANSLATION. By BISHOPS and CLERGY of the
ANGLICAN CHURCH. Edited by Canon F. C. COOK, M.A.

THE OLD TESTAMENT. 6 VOLS. Medium 8vo. 6l. 15s.

Vol. I. 30s.	GENESIE—DEUTERONOMY.	Vol. IV. 24s.	JOB—SONG OF SOLOMON.
Vol. II. 20s.	JOSHUA—KINGS.	Vol. V. 20s. ISAIAH—JEREMIAH.	
Vol. III. 18s.	KINGS II.—ESTHER.	Vol. VI. 25s.	EZEKIEL - MALACHI.

THE NEW TESTAMENT. 4 VOLS. Medium 8vo. 4l. 14s.

Vol. I. 18s.	ST. MATTHEW—ST. LUKE.	Vol. III. 28s.	ROMANS—PHILEMON.
Vol. II. 20s.	ST. JOHN.—ACTS OF THE APOSTLES.	Vol. IV. 28s.	HEBREWS — REVELA-TION.

BIBLE COMMENTARY. THE APOCRYPHA. By Various Writers. Edited by HENRY WACE, D.D. 2 vols. Medium 8vo. 50s.
———————— THE STUDENT'S EDITION. Abridged and Edited by REV. J. M. FULLER, M.A. 6 Vols Crown 8vo. 7s. 6d. each. OLD TESTAMENT. 4 Vols. NEW TESTAMENT. 2 Vols.
BIRD (ISABELLA). Hawaiian Archipelago; or Six Months among the Palm Groves, Coral Reefs, and Volcanoes of the Sandwich Islands. Illustrations. Crown 8vo. 7s. 6d.
———— A Lady's Life in the Rocky Mountains. Illustrations. Post 8vo. 7s. 6d.
———— The Golden Chersonese and the Way Thither. Illustrations. Post 8vo. 14s.
———— Unbeaten Tracks in Japan : Including Visits to the Aborigines of Yezo and the Shrines of Nikko and Isé. Illustrations. Crown 8vo. 7s. 6d.
———— Journeys in Persia and Kurdistan : with a Summer in the Upper Karun Region, and a Visit to the Nestorian Rayahs. Maps and 36 Illustrations. 2 vols. Crown 8vo. 24s.
I ISHOP (MRS.). [See BIRD (ISABELLA).]
BLACKIE (C.). Geographical Etymology; or, Dictionary of Place Names. Third Edition. Crown 8vo. 7s.
BLUNT (REV. J. J.). Undesigned Coincidences in the Writings of the Old and New Testaments, an Argument of their Veracity. Post 8vo. 6s.
———— History of the Christian Church in the First Three Centuries. Post 8vo. 6s.
———— The Parish Priest; His Duties, Acquirements, and Obligations. Post 8vo. 6s.
BOOK OF COMMON PRAYER. Illustrated with Coloured Borders, Initial Letters, and Woodcuts. 8vo. 18s.
BORROW (GEORGE). The Bible in Spain; or, the Journeys and Imprisonments of an Englishman in an attempt to circulate the Scriptures in the Peninsula. Portrait. Post 8vo. 2s. 6d.
———— The Zincali. An Account of the Gipsies of Spain ; Their Manners, Customs, Religion, and Language. 2s. 6d.
———— Lavengro; Scholar—Gypsy—and Priest. 2s. 6d.
———— Romany Rye. A Sequel to Lavengro. Post 8vo. 2s. 6d.
———— WILD WALES : its People, Language, and Scenery. Post 8vo. 2s. 6d.
———— Romano Lavo-Lil. With Illustrations of the English Gypsies; their Poetry and Habitations. Post 8vo. 5s.
BOSWELL'S Life of Samuel Johnson, LL.D. Including the Tour to the Hebrides. Edited by Mr. CROKER. Seventh Edition. Portraits. 1 vol. Medium 8vo. 12s.
BOWEN (LORD JUSTICE). Virgil in English Verse, Eclogues and Æneid, Books I.—VI. Map and Frontispiece. 8vo. 12s.
BRADLEY (DEAN). Arthur Penrhyn Stanley ; Biographical Lectures. Crown 8vo. 8s. 6d.
BREWER (REV. J. S.). The Reign of Henry VIII.; from his Accession till the Death of Wolsey. Illustrated from Original Documents. Edited by JAMES GAIRDNER. With Portrait. 2 vols. 8vo. 30s.
———— The Endowments and Establishment of the Church of England. Edited by L. T. DIBDIN, M.A. Post 8vo. 6s.
BRIDGES (MRS. F. D.). A Lady's Travels in Japan, Thibet, Yarkand, Kashmir, Java, the Straits of Malacca, Vancouver's Island, &c. With Map and Illustrations from Sketches by the Author. Crown 8vo. 15s.

BRITISH ASSOCIATION REPORTS. 8vo.

₊ The Reports for the years 1831 to 1875 may be obtained at the Offices of the British Association.

Glasgow, 1876, 25s.
Plymouth, 1877, 24s.
Dublin, 1878, 24s.
Sheffield, 1879, 24s.
Swansea, 1880, 24s.
York, 1881, 24s.

Southampton, 1882, 24s.
Southport, 1883, 24s.
Canada, 1884, 24s.
Aberdeen, 1885, 24s.
Birmingham, 1886, 24s.
Manchester, 1887, 24s.

Bath, 1888, 24s.
Newcastle-upon-Tyne, 1889, 24s.
Leeds, 1890, 24s.
Cardiff, 1891, 24s.

BROADFOOT (MAJOR W., R.E.) Services in Afghanistan, the Punjab, and on the N. W. Frontier of India. Compiled from his papers and those of Lords Ellenborough and Hardinge. Maps. 8vo. 15s.

BROCKLEHURST (T. U.). Mexico To-day: A Country with a Great Future. With a Glance at the Prehistoric Remains and Antiquities of the Montezumas. Plates and Woodcuts. Medium 8vo. 21s.

BRUCE (Hon. W. N.). Life of Sir Charles Napier. [See NAPIER.]

BRUGSCH (PROFESSOR). A History of Egypt under the Pharaohs. Derived entirely from Monuments. A New and t' oroughly Revised Edition. Edited by M. BRODRICK. Maps. 1 Vol. 8vo. 18s.

BULGARIA. [See BARKLEY, HUHN, MINCHIN.]

BUNBURY (SIR E. H.). A History of Ancient Geography, among the Greeks and Romans, from the Earliest Ages till the Fall of the Roman Empire. Maps. 2 Vols. 8vo. 21s.

BURBIDGE (F. W.). The Gardens of the Sun: or A Naturalist's Journal in Borneo and the Sulu Archipelago. Illustrations. Cr. 8vo. 14s.

BURCKHARDT'S Cicerone; or Art Guide to Painting in Italy. New Edition, revised by J. A. CROWE. Post 8vo. 6s.

BURGES (SIR JAMES BLAND, BART.) Selections from his Letters and Papers, as Under-Secretary of State for Foreign Affairs. With Notices of his Life. Edited by JAMES HUTTON. 8vo. 15s.

BURGON (DEAN). A Biography. Illustrated by Extracts from his Letters and Early Journals. By E. MEYRICK GOULBURN, D.D. Portraits. 2 Vols. 8vo. 24s.

——— The Revision Revised : (1.) The New Greek Text; (2.) The New English Version; (3.) Westcott and Hort's Textual Theory. Second Edition. 8vo. 14s.

——— Lives of Twelve Good Men. Martin J. Routh, H. J. Rose, Chas. Marriott, Edward Hawkins, Saml. Wilberforce, R. L. Cotton, Richard Gresswell, H. O. Coxe, H. L. Mansel, Wm. Jacobson, C. P. Eden, C. L. Higgins. New Edition. With Portraits. 1 Vol. 8vo. 16s.

BURN (COL.). Dictionary of Naval and Military Technical Terms, English and French—French and English. Crown 8vo. 15s.

BUTTMANN'S LEXILOGUS; a Critical Examination of the Meaning of numerous Greek Words, chiefly in Homer and Hesiod. By Rev. J. R. FISHLAKE. 8vo. 12s.

BUXTON (CHARLES). Memoirs of Sir Thomas Fowell Buxton, Bart. Portrait. 8vo. 16s. *Popular Edition.* Fcap. 8vo. 5s.

——— Notes of Thought. With a Biographical Notice. *Second Edition.* Post 8vo. 5s.

——— (SYDNEY C.). A Handbook to the Political Questions of the Day: with the Arguments on Either Side. Eighth Edition. 8vo. 10s. 6d.

——— Finance and Politics, an Historical Study. 1783-1885. 2 Vols. 28s.

——— Handbook to the Death Duties. Post 8vo. 3s. 6d.

BYRON'S (Lord) LIFE AND WORKS :—
  LIFE, LETTERS, AND JOURNALS. By THOMAS MOORE. One
    Volume, Portraits. Royal 8vo. 7s. 6d.
  LIFE AND POETICAL WORKS. *Popular Edition.* Portraits.
    2 Vols. Royal 8vo. 15s.
  POETICAL WORKS. *Library Edition.* Portrait. 6 Vols. 8vo. 45s.
  POETICAL WORKS. *Cabinet Edition.* Plates. 10 Vols. 12mo. 30s.
  POETICAL WORKS. *Pocket Ed.* 8 Vols. 16mo. In a case. 21s.
  POETICAL WORKS. *Popular Edition.* Plates. Royal 8vo. 7s. 6d.
  POETICAL WORKS. *Pearl Edition.* Crown 8vo. 2s. 6d. Cloth.
    3s. 6d.
  CHILDE HAROLD. With 80 Engravings. Crown 8vo. 12s.
  CHILDE HAROLD. 16mo. 2s. 6d.
  CHILDE HAROLD. Vignettes. 16mo. 1s.
  CHILDE HAROLD. Portrait. 16mo. 6d.
  TALES AND POEMS. 16mo. 2s. 6d.
  MISCELLANEOUS. 2 Vols. 16mo. 5s.
  DRAMAS AND PLAYS. 2 Vols. 16mo. 5s.
  DON JUAN AND BEPPO. 2 Vols. 16mo. 5s.

CAILLARD (E. M.). Electricity; The Science of the 19th
  Century. A Sketch for General Readers. With Illustrations. Crown
  8vo. 7s. 6d.
——————————— The Invisible Powers of Nature. Some
  Elementary Lessons in Physical Science for Beginners. Post 8vo. 6s.

CALDECOTT (ALFRED). English Colonization and Empire.
  Coloured Maps and Plans. Crown 8vo. 3s. 6d. (Univ. Extension Series.)

CAMPBELL (LORD). Autobiography, Journals and Correspon-
  dence. By Mrs. Hardcastle. Portrait. 2 Vols. 8vo. 30s.
——————————— Lord Chancellors and Keepers of the Great
  Seal of England. From the Earliest Times to the Death of Lord Eldon
  in 1838. 10 Vols. Crown 8vo. 6s. each.
— - -- -- - —. Chief Justices of England. From the Norman
  Conquest to the Death of Lord Tenterden. 4 Vols. Crown 8vo. 6s. each.
——————————— (THOS.) Essay on English Poetry. With Short
  Lives of the British Poets. Post 8vo. 3s. 6d.

CAREY (Life of). [See GEORGE SMITH.]

CARLISLE (BISHOP OF). Walks in the Regions of Science and
  Faith—a Series of Essays. Crown 8vo. 7s. 6d.
——————————— The Foundations of the Creed. Being a Discussion
  of the Grounds upon which the Articles of the Apostles' Creed may be
  held by Earnest and Thoughtful Minds in the 19th Century. 8vo. 14s.

CARNARVON (LORD). Portugal, Gallicia, and the Basque
  Provinces. Post 8vo. 3s. 6d.

CAVALCASELLE'S WORKS. [See CROWE.]

CESNOLA (GEN.). Cyprus; its Ancient Cities, Tombs, and Temples. With 400 Illustrations. Medium 8vo. 50s.

CHAMBERS (G. F.). A Practical and Conversational Pocket
  Dictionary of the English, French, and German Languages. Designed
  for Travellers and Students generally. Small 8vo. 6s.

CHILD-CHAPLIN (Dr.). Benedicite; or, Song of the Three Children;
  being Illustrations of the Power, Beneficence, and Des'gn manifested
  by the Creator in his Works. Post 8vo. 6s.

CHISHOLM (Mrs.). Perils of the Polar Seas; True Stories of
  Arctic Discovery and Adventure. Illustrations. Post 8vo. 6s.

CHURTON (ARCHDEACON). Poetical Remains. Post 8vo. 7s. 6d.

CLARKE (MAJOR G. SYDENHAM), Royal Engineers. Fortification; I.s Past Achievements, Recent Development, and Future Progress. With Illustrations. Medium 8vo. 21s.

CLASSIC PREACHERS OF THE ENGLISH CHURCH. Lectures delivered at St. James'. 2 Vols. Post 8vo. 7s. 6d. each.

CLEVELAND (DUCHESS OF). The Battle Abbey Roll. With some account of the Norman Lineages. 3 Vols. Sm. 4to. 48s.

CLIVE'S (LORD) Life. By REV. G. R. GLEIG. Post 8vo. 3s. 6d.

CLODE (C. M.). Military Forces of the Crown; their Administration and Government. 2 Vols. 8vo. 21s. each.

—————— Administration of Justice under Military and Martial Law, as applicable to the Army, Navy, and Auxiliary Forces. 8vo. 12s

COLEBROOKE (SIR EDWARD, BART.). Life of the Hon. Mountstuart Elphinstone. With Portrait and Plans. 2 Vols. 8vo. 26s.

COLERIDGE (SAMUEL TAYLOR), and the English Romantic School. By PROF. BRANDL. With Portrait, Crown 8vo. 12s.

—————— Table-Talk. Portrait. 12mo. 3s. 6d.

COLES (JOHN). Summer Travelling in Iceland. With a Chapter on Askja. BY E. D. MORGAN. Map and Illustrations. 18s.

COLLINS (J. CHURTON). BOLINGBROKE: an Historical Study. With an Essay on Voltaire in England. Crown 8vo. 7s. 6d.

COLONIAL LIBRARY. [See Home and Colonial Library.]

COOK (Canon F. C.). The Revised Version of the Three First Gospels, considered in its Bearings upon the Record of Our Lord's Words and Incidents in His Life. 8vo. 9s.

—————— The Origins of Language and Religion. 8vo. 15s.

COOKE (E. W.). Leaves from my Sketch-Book. With Descriptive Text. 50 Plates. 2 Vols. Small folio. 31s. 6d. each.

—————— (W. H.). History and Antiquities of the County of Hereford. Vol. III. In continuation of Duncumb's History. 4to. £2 12s. 6d.

—————— Additions to Duncumb's History. Vol. II. 4to. 15s.

—————— The Hundred of Grimsworth. Parts I. and II. 4to. 17s. 6d. each.

COOKERY (MODERN DOMESTIC). Adapted for Private Families. By a Lady. Woodcuts. Fcap. 8vo. 5s.

COOLEY (THOMAS M.). [See AMERICA, RAILWAYS OF.]

CORNEY GRAIN. By Himself. Post 8vo. 1s.

COURTHOPE (W. J.). The Liberal Movement in English Literature. A Series of Essays. Post 8vo. 6s.

—————— Life and Works of Alexander Pope. With Portraits. 10 Vols. 8vo. 10s. 6d. each.

CRABBE (REV. G.). Life & Works. Illustrations. Royal 8vo. 7s.

CRAIK (HENRY). Life of Jonathan Swift. Portrait. 8vo. 18s.

CRIPPS (WILFRED). Old English Plate: Ecclesiastical, Decorative, and Domestic, its Makers and Marks. New Edition. With Illustrations and 2016 facsimile Plate Marks. Medium 8vo. 21s.
*** Tables of the Date Letters and Marks sold separately. 5s.

CROKER (RT. HON. J. W.). Correspondence and Journals, relating to the Political and Social Events of the first half of the present Century. Edited by LOUIS J. JENNINGS, M.P. Portrait. 3 Vols. 8vo. 43s.

—————— Progressive Geography for Children. 18mo. 1s 6d.

CROKER (Rt. Hon. J. W.). Boswell's Life of Johnson. [See Boswell.]
———— Historical Essay on the Guillotine. Fcap. 8vo. 1s.
CROWE and CAVALCASELLE. Lives of the Early Flemish
Painters. Woodcuts. Post 8vo. 7s. 6d.; or Large Paper 8vo, 15s.
———— Life and Times of Titian, with some Account of his
Family. Illustrations. 2 Vols. 8vo. 21s.
———— Raphael; His Life and Works. 2 Vols. 8vo. 33s.
CUMMING (R. Gordon). Five Years of a Hunter's Life in the
Far Interior of South Africa. Woodcuts. Post 8vo. 6s.
CUNDILL (Colonel J. P.), R.A., and HAKE (C. Napier). Re-
searches on the Power of Explosives. Translated and Condensed from
the French of M. Berthelot. With Illustrations. 8vo.
CUNNINGHAM (Prof. W.), D.D. The Use and Abuse of Money.
Crown 8vo. 2s. (University Extension Series.)
CURRIE (C. L.). An Argument for the Divinity of Jesus Christ.
Translated from the French of the Abbé Em. Bougaud. Post 8vo. 6s.
CURTIUS' (Professor) Student's Greek Grammar, for the Upper
Forms. Edited by Dr. Wm. Smith. Post 8vo. 6s.
————Elucidations of the above Grammar. Translated by
Evelyn Abbot. Post 8vo. 7s. 6d.
———— Smaller Greek Grammar for the Middle and Lower
Forms. Abridged from the larger work. 12mo. 3s. 6d.
———— Accidence of the Greek Language. Extracted from
the above work. 12mo. 2s. 6d.
———— Principles of Greek Etymology. Translated by A. S.
Wilkins and E. B. England. New Edition. 2 Vols. 8vo. 28s.
———— The Greek Verb, its Structure and Development.
Translated by A. S. Wilkins, and E. B. England. 8vo. 12s.
CURZON (Hon. Robert). Visits to the Monasteries of the Levant.
Illustrations. Post 8vo. 7s. 6d.
CUST (General). Warriors of the 17th Century—Civil Wars of
France and England. 2 Vols. 16s. Commanders of Fleets and Armies.
2 Vols. 18s.
———— Annals of the Wars—18th & 19th Century.
With Maps. 9 Vols. Post 8vo. 5s. each.
DAVY (Sir Humphry). Consolations in Travel; or, Last Days
of a Philosopher. Woodcuts. Fcap. 8vo. 3s. 6d.
———— Salmonia; or, Days of Fly Fishing. Woodcuts.
Fcap. 8vo. 3s. 6d.
DE COSSON (Major E. A.). The Cradle of the Blue Nile; a
Journey through Abyssinia and Soudan. Map and Illustrations.
2 Vols. Post 8vo. 21s.
———— Days and Nights of Service with Sir Gerald Graham's
Field Force at Suakim. Plan and Illustrations. Crown 8vo. 14s.
DENNIS (George). The Cities and Cemeteries of Etruria.
20 Plans and 200 Illustrations. 2 Vols. Medium 8vo. 21s.
———— (Robert). Industrial Ireland. Suggestions for a Prac-
tical Policy of "Ireland for the Irish." Crown 8vo. 6s.
DARWIN'S (Charles) Life and Letters, with an autobiographical
Chapter. Edited by his Son, Francis Darwin, F.R.S. Portraits.
3 Vols. 8vo. 36s.
———— Biography, founded on the above work. By
Francis Darwin. 1 Vol. Crown 8vo.
———— An Illustrated Edition of the Voyage of a
Naturalist round the World in H.M.S. Beagle. With Views of Places
Visited and Described. By R. T. Pritchett. 100 Illustrations.
Medium 8vo. 21s.

DARWIN (CHARLES) *continued.*

JOURNAL OF A NATURALIST DURING A VOYAGE ROUND THE WORLD. Popular Edition. With Portrait. 8s. 6d.

ORIGIN OF SPECIES BY MEANS OF NATURAL SELECTION. Library Edition. 2 vols. 12s.; or popular Edition. 6s.

DESCENT OF MAN, AND SELECTION IN. RELATION TO SEX. Woodcuts. Library Ed. 2 vols. 15s.; or popular Ed. 7s. 6d.

VARIATION OF ANIMALS AND PLANTS UNDER DOMESTICATION. Woodcuts. 2 Vols. 15s.

EXPRESSIONS OF THE EMOTIONS IN MAN AND ANIMALS. With Illustrations. 12s.

VARIOUS CONTRIVANCES BY WHICH ORCHIDS ARE FERTILIZED BY INSECTS. Woodcuts. 7s. 6d.

MOVEMENTS AND HABITS OF CLIMBING PLANTS. Woodcuts. 6s.

INSECTIVOROUS PLANTS. Woodcuts. 9s.

CROSS AND SELF-FERTILIZATION IN THE VEGETABLE KINGDOM. 9s.

DIFFERENT FORMS OF FLOWERS ON PLANTS OF THE SAME SPECIES. 7s. 6d.

POWER OF MOVEMENT IN PLANTS. Woodcuts.

THE FORMATION OF VEGETABLE MOULD THROUGH THE ACTION OF WORMS. Illustrations. Post 8vo. 6s.

FACTS AND ARGUMENTS FOR DARWIN. By FRITZ MULLER. Woodcuts. Post 8vo. 6s.

DERBY (EARL OF). Iliad of Homer rendered into English Blank Verse. With Portrait. 2 Vols. Post 8vo. 10s.

DERRY (BISHOP OF). Witness of the Psalms to Christ and Christianity. Crown 8vo. 9s.

DICEY (PROF. A. V.). England's Case against Home Rule. Crown 8vo. 7s. 6d.

———— Why England Maintains the Union. A popular rendering of the above. By C. E. S. Fcap. 8vo. 1s.

DOG-BREAKING. [See HUTCHINSON.]

DÖLLINGER (DR.). Studies in European History, being Academical Addresses. Translated by MARGARET WARRE. Portrait. 8vo. 14s.

DRAKE'S (SIR FRANCIS) Life, Voyages, and Exploits, by Sea and Land. By JOHN BARROW. Post 8vo. 2s.

DRINKWATER (JOHN). History of the Siege of Gibraltar, 1779-1783. With a Description of that Garrison. Post 8vo. 2s.

DU CHAILLU (PAUL B.). Land of the Midnight Sun; Illustrations. 2 Vols. 8vo. 36s.

———————— The Viking Age. The Early History, Manners, and Customs of the Ancestors of the English-speaking Nations. With 1,300 Illustrations. 2 Vols. 8vo. 42s.

———————— Equatorial Africa and Ashango Land. Adventures in the Great Forest of Equatorial Africa, and the Country of the Dwarfs. Popular Edition. With Illustrations. Post 8vo. 7s. 6d.

DUFFERIN (LORD). Letters from High Latitudes ; a Yacht Voyage to Iceland. Woodcuts. Post 8vo. 7s. 6d.

———————— Speeches in India, 1884—8. 8vo. 9s.

———————— (LADY). Our Viceregal Life in India, 1884—1888. Portrait. Post 8vo. 7s. 6d.

———————— My Canadian Journal, 1872—78. Extracts from Home Letters written while Ld. Dufferin was Gov.-Gen. Portraits, Map, and Illustrations. Crown 8vo. 12s. 100 Large Paper Copies, 1l. 1s. each.

DUNCAN (Col.). English in Spain; or, The Story of the War of Succession, 1834-1840. 8vo. 16s.

DÜRER (Albert); his Life and Work. By Dr. Thausing. Edited by F. A. Eaton. Illustrations. 2 Vols. Medium 8vo. 42s.

EARLE (Professor John). The Psalter of 1539 : A Landmark of English Literature. Compr sing the Text, in Black Letter Type. With Notes. Square 8vo.

EASTLAKE (Sir C.). Contributions to the Literature of the Fine Arts. With Memoir by Lady Eastlake. 2 Vols. 8vo. 24s.

EDWARDS (W. H.). Voyage up the River Amazon, including a Visit to Para. Post 8vo. 2s.

ELLESMERE (Lord). Two Sieges of Vienna by the Turks. Post 8vo. 2s.

ELLIOT (Mrs Minto). The Diary of an Idle Woman in Constantin ple Crown 8vo.

ELLIS (W.). Madagascar Revisited. 8vo. 16s.

———— Memoir. By His Son. Portrait. 8vo. 10s. 6d.

———— (Robinson). Poems and Fragments of Catullus. 16mo. 5s.

ELPHINSTONE (Hon. M.). History of India—the Hindoo and Mahommedan Periods. Edited by Professor Cowell. Map. 8vo. 18s.

———————— Rise of the British Power in the East. A Continuation of his History of India in the Hindoo and Mahommedan Periods. Maps. 8vo. 16s.

——————— - Life of. [See Colebrooke.]

—————————— (H. W.). Patterns for Ornamental Turning. Illustrations. Small 4to. 15s.

ELTON (Capt.). Adventures among the Lakes and Mountains of Eastern and Central Africa. Illustrations. 8vo 21s.

ELWIN (Rev. Warwick). The Minister of Baptism. A History of Church Opinion from the time of the Apostles, especially with reference to Heretical and Lay Administration. 8vo. 1?s.

ENGLAND. [See Arthur—Brewer—Croker—Hume—Markham —Smith—and Stanhope.]

ESSAYS ON CATHEDRALS. Edited by Dean Howson. 8vo. 12s.

ETON LATIN GRAMMAR. For use in the Upper Forms. By F. H. Rawlins, M.A., and W. R. Inge, M.A. Crown 8vo. 6s.

—————— ELEMENTARY LATIN GRAMMAR. For use in the Lower Forms. Compiled by A. C. Ainger, M.A., and H. G. Wintle, M.A. Crown 8vo. 3s. 6d.

—————— PREPARATORY ETON GRAMMAR. Abridged from the above Work. By the same Editors. Crown 8vo. 2s.

—————— FIRST LATIN EXERCISE BOOK, adapted to the Elementary and Preparatory Grammars. By the same Editors. Crown 8vo. 2s. 6d.

—————— FOURTH FORM OVID. Selections from Ovid and Tibullus. With Notes by H. G. Wintle. Post 8vo. 2s. 6d.

ETON HORACE. The Odes, Epodes, and Carmen Sæculare. With Notes. By F. W. Cornish, M.A. Maps. Crown 8vo. 6s.

—————— EXERCISES IN ALGEBRA, by E. P. Rouse, M.A., and Arthur Cockshott, M.A. Crown 8vo. 3s.

—————— ARITHMETIC. By Rev. T. Dalton, M.A. Crown 8vo. 3s.

EXPLOSIVES. [See Cundill.]

FERGUSSON (James). History of Architecture in all Countries from the Earliest Times. A New and thoroughly Revised Edition. With 1,700 Illustrations. 5 Vols. Medium 8vo Vols. I. & II. Ancient and Mediæval. Edited by Phené Spiers. III. Indian & Eastern. 31s. 6d. IV. Modern. 2 vols. 31s. 6d.

FITZGERALD (Bishop). Lectures on Ecclesiastical History, including the origin and progress of the English Reformation, from Wicliffe to the Great Rebellion. With a Memoir. 2 Vols. 8vo. 21*s.*

FITZPATRICK (WILLIAM J.). The Correspondence of Daniel O'Connell, the Liberator. With Portrait. 2 Vols. 8vo. 36*s.*

FLEMING (PROFESSOR). Student's Manual of Moral Philosophy. With Quotations and References. Post 8vo. 7*s.* 6*d.*

FLOWER GARDEN. By REV. THOS. JAMES. Fcap. 8vo. 1*s.*

FORD (ISABELLA O.). Miss Blake of Monkshalton. A Novel. Crown 8vo. 5*s.*

FORD (RICHARD). Gatherings from Spain. Post 8vo. 3*s.* 6*d.*

FORSYTH (WILLIAM). Hortensius; an Historical Essay on the Office and Duties of an Advocate. Illustrations. 8vo. 7*s.* 6*d.*

FORTIFICATION. [See CLARKE.]

FRANCE (HISTORY OF). [See ARTHUR—MARKHAM—SMITH—STUDENTS'—TOCQUEVILLE.]

FREAM (W.), LL.D. Elements of Agriculture; a text-book prepared under the authority of the Royal Agricultural Society of England. With 200 Illustrations. Crown 8vo. 2*s.* 6*d.*

FRENCH IN ALGIERS; The Soldier of the Foreign Legion—and the Prisoners of Abd-el-Kadir. Post 8vo. 2*s.*

FRERE (MARY). Old Deccan Days, or Hindoo Fairy Legends current in Southern India, with Introduction by Sir BARTLE FRERE. With Illustrations. Post 8vo. 5*s.*

GALTON (F.). Art of Travel; or, Hints on the Shifts and Contrivances available in Wild Countries. Woodcuts. Post 8vo. 7*s.* 6*d.*

GAMBIER PARRY (T.). The Ministry of Fine Art to the Happiness of Life. Revised Edition, with an Index. 8vo. 14*s.*

———— **(MAJOR).** The Combat with Suffering. Fcap. 8vo. 3*s.* 6*d.*

GARDNER (PROF. PERCY). New Chapters in Greek History. Historical results of recent excavations in Greece and Asia Minor. With Illustrations. 8vo. 15*s.*

GEOGRAPHY. [See BUNBURY—CROKER—RAMSAY—RICHARDSON—SMITH—STUDENTS'.]

GEOGRAPHICAL SOCIETY'S JOURNAL. (1846 to 1881.) SUPPLEMENTARY PAPERS. Royal 8vo.

Vol. I., Part i. Travels and Researches in Western China. By E. COLBORNE BABER. Maps. 5*s.*

Part ii.—1. Recent Geography of Central Asia; from Russian Sources. By E. DELMAR MORGAN. 2. Progress of Discovery on the Coasts of New Guinea. By C. B. MARKHAM. Bibliographical Appendix, by E. C Rye. Maps. 5*s.*

Part iii.—1. Report on Part of the Ghilzi Country, &c. By Lieut. J. S. BROADFOOT. 2. Journey from Shiraz to Jashk. By J. R. PREECE. 2*s.* 6*d.*

Part iv.—Geographical Education. By J. S. KELTIE. 2*s.* 6*d.*

Vol. II., Part i. —1. Exploration in S. and S.W. China. By A. R. COLQUHOUN. 2. Bibliography and Cartography of Hispaniola. By H. LING ROTH. 3. Explorations in Zanzibar Dominions by Lieut. C. STEWART SMITH, R.N. 2*s.* 6*d.*

Part ii.—A Bibliography of Algeria, from the Expedition of Charles V. in 1541 to 1887 By SIR R. L. PLAYFAIR. 4*s.*

Part iii.—1. On the Measurement of Heights by the Barometer. By JOHN BALL, F.R.S. 2. River Entrances. By HUGH ROBERT MILL. 3 Mr. J.F. Needham's Journey in South Eastern Tibet.

Part iv.—1. The Bibliography of the Barbary States. Part i. By SIR R. L. PLAYFAIR. 2. Hudson's Bay and Strait. By Commodore A. H. MARKHAM, R.N.

Vol. III, Part i.—Journey of Carey and Dalgleish in Chinese Turkestan and Northern Tibet; and General Prejevalsky on the Orography of Northern Tibet.

GEORGE (ERNEST). The Mosel ; Twenty Etchings. Imperial
4to, 42s.
———— Loire and South of France ; Twenty Etchings. Folio. 42s.
GERMANY (HISTORY OF). [See MARKHAM.]
GIBBON'S History of the Decline and Fall of the Roman Empire.
Edited with notes by MILMAN, GUIZOT, and Dr. WM. SMITH. Maps.
8 Vols. 8vo. 60s. Student's Edition. 7s. 6d. (See STUDENT'S.)
GIFFARD (EDWARD). Deeds of Naval Daring ; or, Anecdotes of
the British Navy. Fcap. 8vo. 3s. 6d.
GILBERT (JOSIAH). Landscape in Art : before the days of Claude
and Salvator. With 150 Illustrations. Medium 8vo. 30s.
GILL (CAPT.). The River of Golden Sand. A Journey through
China to Burmah. Edited by E. C. BABER. With MEMOIR by Col.
YULE, C.B. Portrait, Map, and Illustrations. Post 8vo. 7s. 6d.
———— (MRS.). Six Months in Ascension. An Unscientific Ac-
count of a Scientific Expedition. Map. Crown 8vo. 9s.
GLADSTONE (W. E.). Rome and the Newest Fashions in
Religion. 8vo. 7s. 6d.
——————— Gleanings of Past Years, 1843-78. 7 Vols. Small
8vo. 2s. 6d. each. I. The Throne, the Prince Consort, the Cabinet and
Constitution. II. Personal and Literary. III. Historical and Specu-
lative. IV. Foreign. V. and VI. Ecclesiastical. VII. Miscellaneous.
———— Special Aspects of the Irish Question ; A Series of
Reflections in and since 1886. Collected from various Sources and
Reprinted. Crown 8vo. 3s. 6d.
GLEIG (G. R.). Campaigns of the British Army at Washington
and New Orleans. Post 8vo. 2s.
———— Story of the Battle of Waterloo. Post 8vo. 3s. 6d.
———— Narrative of Sale's Brigade in Affghanistan. Post 8vo. 2s.
———— Life of Lord Clive. Post 8vo. 3s. 6d.
——————— Sir Thomas Munro. Post 8vo. 3s. 6d.
GOLDSMITH'S (OLIVER) Works. Edited with Notes by PETER
CUNNINGHAM. Vignettes. 4 Vols. 8vo. 30s.
GOMM (F.M. SIR WM.). His Letters and Journals. 1799 to
1815. Edited by F.C. Carr Gomm. With Portrait. 8vo. 12s.
GORDON (SIR ALEX.). Sketches of German Life, and Scenes
from the War of Liberation. Post 8vo. 3s. 6d.
———— (LADY DUFF). The Amber-Witch. Post 8vo. 2s.
See also ROSS.
———————— The French in Algiers. Post 8vo. 2s.
GORE (Rev. CHARLES, Edited by). Lux Mundi. A Series of
Studies in the Religion of the Incarnation. By various Writers.
Popular Edition, Crown 8vo. 6s.
———————— The Bampton Lectures, 1891 ; The Incarna-
tion of the Son of God. 8vo. 7s. 6d.
GOULBURN (DEAN). Three Counsels of the Divine Master for
the conduct of the Spiritual Life :—The Commencement ; The
Virtues ; The Conflict. Crown 8vo. 9s.
See also BURGON.
GRAMMARS. [See CURTIUS — ETON—HALL — HUTTON—KING
EDWARD—LEATHES—MAETZNER—MATTHIÆ—SMITH.]
GREECE (HISTORY OF). [See GROTE—SMITH—STUDENTS'.]
GRIFFITH (REV. CHARLES). A History of Strathfieldsaye.
With Illustrations. 4to. 10s. 6d.

GROTE'S (GEORGE) WORKS :—

HISTORY OF GREECE. From the Earliest Times to the Death of Alexander the Great. *New Edition.* Portrait, Map, and Plans. 10 Vols. Post 8vo. 5s. each. (*The Volumes may be had Separately.*)

PLATO, and other Companions of Socrates. 3 Vols. 8vo. 45s.; or, New Edition, Edited by ALEX. BAIN. 4 Vols. Crown 8vo. 5s. each.

ARISTOTLE. 8vo. 12s.

PERSONAL LIFE. Portrait. 8vo. 12s.

MINOR WORKS. Portrait. 8vo. 14s.

———— (MRS.). A Sketch. By LADY EASTLAKE. Crown 8vo. 6s.

GUILLEMARD (F. H.), M.D. The Voyage of the Marchesa to Kamschatka and New Guinea. With Notices of Formosa and the Islands of the Malay Archipelago. New Edition. With Maps and 150 Illustrations. One volume. Medium 8vo. 21s.

HAKE (G. NAPIER) on Explosives. [See CUNDILL.]

HALL'S (T. D.) School Manual of English Grammar. With Illustrations and Practical Exercises. 12mo. 3s. 6d.

———— Primary English Grammar for Elementary Schools. With numerous Exercises, and graduated Parsing Lessons. 16mo. 1s.

———— Manual of English Composition. With Copious Illustrations and Practical Exercises. 12mo. 3s. 6d.

———— Child's First Latin Book, comprising a full Practice of Nouns, Pronouns, and Adjectives, with the Verbs. 16mo. 2s.

HALLAM'S (HENRY) WORKS :—

THE CONSTITUTIONAL HISTORY OF ENGLAND. *Library Edition,* 3 Vols. 8vo. 30s. *Cabinet Edition,* 3 Vols. Post 8vo. 12s. *Student's Edition,* Post 8vo. 7s. 6d.

HISTORY OF EUROPE DURING THE MIDDLE AGES. *Library Edition,* 3 Vols. 8vo. 30s. *Cabinet Edition,* 3 Vols. Post 8vo. 12s. *Student's Edition,* Post 8vo. 7s. 6d.

LITERARY HISTORY OF EUROPE DURING THE 15TH, 16TH, AND 17TH CENTURIES. *Library Edition,* 3 Vols. 8vo. 36s. *Cabinet Edition,* 4 Vols. Post 8vo. 16s. [Portrait. Fcap. 8vo. 3s. 6d.

HART'S ARMY LIST. (*Published Quarterly and Annually.*)

HAY (SIR J. H. DRUMMOND). Western Barbary, its Wild Tribes and Savage Animals. Post 8vo. 2s.

HAYWARD (A.). Sketches of Eminent Statesmen and Writers, 2 Vols. 8vo. 28s.

———— The Art of Dining. Post 8vo. 2s.

———— A Selection from his Correspondence. Edited with an Introductory account of Mr. Hayward's Early Life. By H. E. CARLISLE. 2 vols. Crown 8vo. 24s.

HEAD'S (SIR FRANCIS) WORKS :—

THE ROYAL ENGINEER. Illustrations. 8vo. 12s.

LIFE OF SIR JOHN BURGOYNE. Post 8vo. 1s.

RAPID JOURNEYS ACROSS THE PAMPAS. Post 8vo. 2s.

STOKERS AND POKERS; or, the L. and N. W. R. Post 8vo. 2s.

HEBER'S (BISHOP) Journals in India. 2 Vols. Post 8vo. 7s.

———— Poetical Works. Portrait. Fcap. 8vo. 3s. 6d.

HERODOTUS. A New English Version. Edited, with Notes and Essays by CANON RAWLINSON, SIR H. RAWLINSON and SIR J. G. WILKINSON. Maps and Woodcuts. 4 Vols. 8vo. 48s.

HERRIES (RT. HON. JOHN). Memoir of his Public Life. By his Son, Edward Herries, C.B. 2 Vols. 8vo. 24s.

FOREIGN HAND-BOOKS.

HAND-BOOK—TRAVEL-TALK. English, French, German, and Italian. New and Revised Edition. 18mo. 3s. 6d.

——————— DICTIONARY : English, French, and German. Containing all the words and idiomatic phrases likely to be required by a traveller. Bound in leather. 16mo. 6s.

——————— HOLLAND AND BELGIUM. Map and Plans. 6s.

——————— NORTH GERMANY and THE RHINE,— The Black Forest, the Hartz, Thüringerwald, Saxon Switzerland, Rügen, the Giant Mountains, Taunus, Odenwald, Elsass, and Lothringen. Map and Plans. Post 8vo. 10s.

——————— SOUTH GERMANY AND AUSTRIA,—Wurtemberg, Bavaria, Austria, Tyrol, Styria, Salzburg, the Dolomites, Hungary, and the Danube, from Ulm to the Black Sea. Maps and Plans. Two Parts. Post 8vo. 12s.

——————— SWITZERLAND, Alps of Savoy, and Piedmont In Two Parts. Maps and Plans. Post 8vo. 10s.

——————— FRANCE, Part I. Normandy, Brittany, the French Alps, the Loire, Seine, Garonne, and Pyrenees. Maps and Plans. 7s. 6d.

——————— FRANCE, Part II. Central France, Auvergne, the Cevennes, Burgundy, the Rhone and Saone, Provence, Nimes, Arles, Marseilles, the French Alps, Alsace, Lorraine, Champagne, &c. Maps and Plans. Post 8vo. 7s. 6d.

——————— THE RIVIERA. Provence, Dauphiné. The Alpes Maritimes, Avignon, Nimes, Arles, Marseilles, Toulon, Cannes, Grasse, Nice, Monaco, Mentone, Bordighera, San Remo, Alassio, Savona, &c.; Grenoble, Grande Chartreuse. Maps and Plans. 8vo. 5s.

——————— MEDITERRANEAN — its Principal Islands, Cities, Seaports, Harbours, and Border Lands. For Travellers and Yachtsmen, with nearly 50 Maps and Plans. Two Parts. Post 8vo. 21s.

——————— ALGERIA AND TUNIS. Algiers, Constantine, Oran, Tlemcen, Bougie, Tebessa, Biskra, the Atlas Range. Maps and Plans. Post 8vo. 12s.

——————— PARIS, and Environs. Maps and Plans. 3s. 6d.

——————— SPAIN, Madrid, The Castiles, The Basque Provinces, Leon, The Asturias, Galicia, Estremadura, Andalusia, Ronda, Granada, Murcia, Valencia, Catalonia, Aragon, Navarre, The Balearic Islands, &c. &c. Maps and Plans. Two Parts. Post 8vo. 20s.

——————— PORTUGAL, Lisbon, Oporto, Cintra, Mafra, Madeira, the Azores, Canary Island, &c. Map and Plan. 12s.

——————— NORTH ITALY, Turin, Milan, Cremona, the Italian Lakes, Bergamo, Brescia, Verona, Mantua, Vicenza, Padua, Ferrara, Bologna, Ravenna, Rimini, Placenza, Genoa, the Riviera, Venice, Parma, Modena, and Romagna. Maps and Plans. Post 8vo. 10s.

——————— CENTRAL ITALY, Florence, Lucca, Tuscany, The Marshes, Umbria, &c. Maps and Plans. Two Parts. Post 8vo. 6s.

——————— ROME and its Environs. 50 Maps and Plans. 10s.

——————— SOUTH ITALY AND SICILY, including Naples and its Environs, Pompeii, Herculaneum, Vesuvius; Sorrento, Capri; Amalfi, Pæstum, Pozzuoli, Capua, Taranto, Bari; Brindisi and the Roads from Rome to Naples; Palermo, Messina, Syracuse, Catania &c. Two Parts. Maps. Post 8vo. 12s

——————— NORWAY. Christiania, Bergen, Trondhjem. The Fjelds and Fjords. An entirely new Edition. Maps and Plans. 7s. 6d.

——————— SWEDEN, Stockholm, Upsala, Gothenburg, the Shores of the Baltic, &c. Maps and Plan. Post 8vo. 6s.

14   LIST OF WORKS

HAND-BOOK—DENMARK, Sleswig, Holstein, Copenhagen, Jutland, Iceland. Maps and Plans. Post 8vo. 6s.
——— RUSSIA, St. Petersburg, Moscow, Poland, and Finland. Maps and Plans. Post 8vo. 18s.
——— GREECE, the Ionian Islands, Athens, the Peloponnesus, the Islands of the Ægean Sea. Albania, Thessaly, Macedonia. &c. In Two Parts. Maps, Plans, and Views. Post 8vo. 24s.
——— TURKEY IN ASIA—Constantinople, the Bosphorus, Dardanelles, Brousa, Plain of Troy, Crete, Cyprus, Smyrna, Ephesus, the Seven Churches, Coasts of the Black Sea, Armenia, Euphrates Valley, Route to India, &c. Maps and Plans. Post 8vo.
——— EGYPT. The Course of the Nile through Egypt and Nubia, Alexandria, Cairo, Thebes, Suez Canal, the Pyramids, Sinai, the Fyoom, &c. Maps and Plans. Post 8vo. 15s.
——— HOLY LAND—Syria, Palestine, Moab, Hauran, Syrian Deserts, Jerusalem, Damascus; and Palmyra. Maps and Plans. Post 8vo. 18s. *⁎* Map of Palestine. In a case. 12s.
——— BOMBAY—Poonah, Beejapoor, Kolapoor, Goa, Jubulpoor, Indore, Surat, Baroda, Ahmedabad, Somnauth, Kurrachee, &c. Map and Plans. Post 8vo. 15s.
——— MADRAS—Trichinopoli, Madura, Tinnevelly, Tuticorin, Bangalore, Mysore, The Nilgiris, Wynaad, Ootacamund, Calicut, Hyderabad, Ajanta, Elura Caves, &c. Maps and Plans. Post 8vo. 15s.
——— BENGAL—Calcutta, Orissa, British Burmah, Rangoon, Moulmein, Mandalay, Darjiling, Dacca, Patna, Benares, N.-W. Provinces, Allahabad, Cawnpore, Lucknow, Agra, Gwalior, Naini Tal, Delhi, &c. Maps and Plans. Post 8vo. 20s.
——— THE PANJAB—Amraoti, Indore, Ajmir, Jaypur, Rohtak, Saharanpur, Ambala, Lodiana, Lahore, Kulu, Simla, Sialkot, Peshawar, Rawul Pindi, Attock, Karachi, Sibi, &c. Maps. 15s.
——— INDIA AND CEYLON, including the Provinces of Bengal, Bombay, and Madras (the Punjab, North west Provinces, Rajputana, the Central Provinces, Mysore, &c.), the Native States and Assam. With 55 Maps and Plans of Towns and Buildings. Post 8vo. 15s.
——— JAPAN. Revised and for the most part Rewritten. With 15 Maps. Post 8vo. 15s. net.

ENGLISH HAND-BOOKS.

HAND-BOOK—ENGLAND AND WALES. An Alphabetical Hand-Book. In One Volume. With Map. Post 8vo. 12s.
——— LONDON. Maps and Plans. 16mo. 3s. 6d.
——— ENVIRONS OF LONDON within a circuit of 20 miles. 2 Vols. Crown 8vo. 21s.
——— ST. PAUL'S CATHEDRAL. 20 Woodcuts. 10s. 6d.
——— EASTERN COUNTIES, Chelmsford, Harwich, Colchester, Maldon, Cambridge, Ely, Newmarket, Bury St. Edmunds, Ipswich, Woodbridge, Felixstowe, Lowestoft, Norwich, Yarmouth, Cromer, &c. Maps and Plans. Post 8vo. 12s.
——— CATHEDRALS of Oxford, Peterborough, Norwich, Ely, and Lincoln. With 90 Illustrations. Crown 8vo. 21s.
——— KENT, Canterbury, Dover, Ramsgate, Sheerness, Rochester, Chatham, Woolwich. Maps and Plans. Post 8vo. 7s. 6d.
——— SUSSEX, Brighton, Chichester, Worthing, Hastings, Lewes, Arundel, &c. Maps and Plans. Post 8vo. 6s.

HAND-BOOK—SURREY AND HANTS, Kingston, Croydon, Reigate, Guildford, Dorking, Winchester, Southampton, New Forest, Portsmouth, ISLE OF WIGHT. &c. Maps and Plans. Post 8vo. 10s.

———— BERKS, BUCKS, AND OXON, Windsor, Eton, Reading, Aylesbury, Uxbridge, Wycombe, Henley, Oxford, Blenheim, the Thames, &c. Maps and Plans. Post 8vo. 9s.

———— WILTS, DORSET, AND SOMERSET, Salisbury, Chippenham, Weymouth, Sherborne, Wells, Bath, Bristol, Taunton, &c. Map. Post 8vo. 12s.

———— DEVON, Exeter, Ilfracombe, Linton, Sidmouth, Dawlish, Teignmouth, Plymouth, Devonport, Torquay. Maps and Plans. Post 8vo. 7s. 6d.

———— CORNWALL, Launceston, Penzance, Falmouth, the Lizard, Land's End, &c. Maps. Post 8vo. 6s.

———— CATHEDRALS of Winchester, Salisbury, Exeter, Wells, Chichester, Rochester, Canterbury, and St. Albans. With 130 Illustrations. 2 Vols. Crown 8vo. 36s. St. Albans separately. 6s.

———— GLOUCESTER, HEREFORD, AND WORCESTER, Cirencester, Cheltenham, Stroud, Tewkesbury, Leominster, Ross, Malvern, Kidderminster, Dudley, Evesham, &c. Map. Post 8vo. 9s.

———— CATHEDRALS of Bristol, Gloucester, Hereford, Worcester, and Lichfield. With 50 Illustrations. Crown 8vo. 16s.

———— NORTH WALES, Bangor, Carnarvon, Beaumaris, Snowdon, Llanberis, Dolgelly, Conway, &c. Maps. Post 8vo. 7s.

———— SOUTH WALES, Monmouth, Llandaff, Merthyr, Vale of Neath, Pembroke, Carmarthen, Tenby, Swansea, The Wye, &c. Map. Post 8vo. 7s.

———— CATHEDRALS OF BANGOR, ST. ASAPH, Llandaff, and St. David's. With Illustrations. Post 8vo. 15s.

———— NORTHAMPTONSHIRE AND RUTLAND— Northampton, Peterborough, Towcester, Daventry, Market Harborough, Kettering, Wellingborough, Thrapston, Stamford, Uppingham, Oakham. Maps. Post 8vo. 7s. 6d.

———— DERBY, NOTTS, LEICESTER, STAFFORD, Matlock, Bakewell, Chatsworth, The Peak, Buxton, Hardwick, Dove Dale, Ashborne, Southwell, Mansfield, Retford, Burton, Belvoir, Melton Mowbray, Wolverhampton, Lichfield, Walsall. Tamworth. Map. Post 8vo.

———— SHROPSHIRE AND CHESHIRE, Shrewsbury, Ludlow, Bridgnorth, Oswestry, Chester, Crewe, Alderley, Stockport, Birkenhead. Maps and Plans. Post 8vo. 6s.

———— LANCASHIRE, Warrington, Bury, Manchester, Liverpool, Burnley, Clitheroe, Bolton, Blackburne, Wigan, Preston, Rochdale, Lancaster, Southport, Blackpool, &c. Maps & Plans. Post 8vo. 7s. 6d.

———— THE ENGLISH LAKES, in Cumberland, Westmoreland, and Lancashire; Lancaster, Furness Abbey, Ambleside, Kendal, Windermere, Coniston, Keswick, Grasmere, Ulswater, Carlisle, Cockermouth, Penrith, Appleby, &c. Maps. Post 8vo. 7s. 6d.

———— YORKSHIRE, Doncaster, Hull, Selby, Beverley, Scarborough, Whitby, Harrogate, Ripon, Leeds, Wakefield, Bradford, Halifax, Huddersfield, Sheffield. Map and Plans. Post 8vo. 12s.

———— CATHEDRALS of York, Ripon, Durham, Carlisle, Chester, and Manchester. With 60 Illustrations. 2 Vols. Cr. 8vo. 21s.

———— DURHAM AND NORTHUMBERLAND, Newcastle, Darlington, Stockton, Hartlepool, Shields, Berwick-on-Tweed, Morpeth, Tynemouth, Coldstream, Alnwick, &c. Map. Post 8vo. 10s.

———— LINCOLNSHIRE, Grantham, Lincoln, Stamford, Sleaford, Spalding, Gainsborough, Grimsby, Boston. Maps and Plans. Post 8vo. 7s. 6d.

———— WARWICKSHIRE. Map. Post 8vo.

———— HERTS, BEDS AND HUNTS.

HAND-BOOK—SCOTLAND, Edinburgh, Melrose, Kelso, Glasgow, Dumfries, Ayr, Stirling, Arran, The Clyde, Oban, Inverary, Loch Lomond, Loch Katrine and Trossachs, Caledonian Canal, Inverness, Perth, Dundee, Aberdeen, Braemar, Skye, Caithness, Ross, Sutherland, &c. Maps and Plans. Post 8vo. 9s.

———— IRELAND, Dublin, Belfast, the Giant's Causeway, Donegal, Galway, Wexford, Cork, Limerick, Waterford, Killarney, Bantry, Glengariff, &c. Maps and Plans. Post 8vo. 10s.

HICKSON (DR. SYDNEY J.). A Naturalist in North Celebes; a Narrative of Travels in Minahassa, the Sangir and Talaut Islands, with Notices of the Fauna, Flora, and Ethnology of the Districts visited. Map and Illustrations. 8vo. 16s.

HISLOP (STEPHEN). [See SMITH, GEORGE.]

HOBSON (J. A.). [See MUMMERY.]

HOLLWAY (J. G.). A Month in Norway. Fcap. 8vo. 2s.

HONEY BEE. By REV. THOMAS JAMES. Fcap. 8vo. 1s.

HOOK (DEAN). Church Dictionary. A Manual of Reference for Clergymen and Students. New Edition, thoroughly revised. Edited by WALTER HOOK, M.A., and W. R. W. STEPHENS, M.A. Med. 8vo. 21s.

———— (THEODORE) Life. By J. G. LOCKHART. Fcap. 8vo. 1s.

HOPE (A. J. BERESFORD). Worship in the Church of England. 8vo, 9s.; or, Popular Selections from, 8vo, 2s. 6d.

———— WORSHIP AND ORDER. 8vo. 9s.

HOPE-SCOTT (JAMES), Memoir. [See ORNSBY.]

HORACE; a New Edition of the Text. Edited by DEAN MILMAN. With 100 Woodcuts. Crown 8vo. 7s. 6d.

———— [See ETON.]

HOUGHTON'S (LORD) Monographs. Portraits. 10s. 6d.

———— POETICAL WORKS. Portrait. 2 Vols. 12s.

———— (ROBERT LORD) Stray Verses, 1889-90. Crown 8vo. 6s.

HOME AND COLONIAL LIBRARY. A Series of Works adapted for all circles and classes of Readers, having been selected for their acknowledged interest, and ability of the Authors. Post 8vo. Published at 2s. and 3s. 6d. each, and arranged under two distinctive heads as follows:—

CLASS A.

HISTORY, BIOGRAPHY, AND HISTORIC TALES.

SIEGE OF GIBRALTAR. By JOHN DRINKWATER. 2s.

THE AMBER-WITCH. By LADY DUFF GORDON. 2s.

CROMWELL AND BUNYAN. By ROBERT SOUTHEY. 2s.

LIFE OF SIR FRANCIS DRAKE. By JOHN BARROW. 2s.

CAMPAIGNS AT WASHINGTON. By REV. G. R. GLEIG. 2s.

THE FRENCH IN ALGIERS. By LADY DUFF GORDON. 2s.

THE FALL OF THE JESUITS. 2s.

LIFE OF CONDÉ. By LORD MAHON. 3s. 6d.

SALE'S BRIGADE. By REV. G. R. GLEIG. 2s.

THE SIEGES OF VIENNA. By LORD ELLESMERE. 2s.

THE WAYSIDE CROSS. By CAPT. MILMAN. 2s.

SKETCHES OF GERMAN LIFE. By SIR A. GORDON. 3s. 6d.

THE BATTLE OF WATERLOO. By REV. G. R. GLEIG. 3s. 6d.

AUTOBIOGRAPHY OF STEFFENS. 2s.

THE BRITISH POETS. By THOMAS CAMPBELL. 3s. 6d.

HISTORICAL ESSAYS. By LORD MAHON. 3s. 6d.

LIFE OF LORD CLIVE. By REV. G. R. GLEIG. 3s. 6d.

NORTH WESTERN RAILWAY. By SIR F. B. HEAD. 2s.

LIFE OF MUNRO. By REV. G. R. GLEIG. 3s. 6d.

CLASS B.
VOYAGES, TRAVELS, AND ADVENTURES.

JOURNALS IN INDIA. By
BISHOP HEBER. 2 Vols. 7s.
TRAVELS IN THE HOLY LAND.
By IRBY and MANGLES. 2s.
MOROCCO AND THE MOORS.
By J. DRUMMOND HAY. 2s.
LETTERS FROM THE BALTIC.
By A LADY. 2s.
NEW SOUTH WALES By MRS.
MEREDITH. 2s.
THE WEST INDIES. By M. G.
LEWIS. 2s.
SKETCHES OF PERSIA. By
SIR JOHN MALCOLM. 3s. 6d.
MEMOIRS OF FATHER RIPA.
2s.
TYPEE AND OMOO. By
HERMANN MELVILLE. 2 Vols. 7s.
MISSIONARY LIFE IN CAN-
ADA. By REV. J. ABBOTT. 2s.
LETTERS FROM MADRAS. By
A LADY. 2s.

HIGHLAND SPORTS. By
CHARLES ST. JOHN. 3s. 6d.
PAMPAS JOURNEYS. By
F. B. HEAD. 2s.
GATHERINGS FROM SPAIN.
By RICHARD FORD. 3s. 6d.
THE RIVER AMAZON. By
W. H. EDWARDS. 2s.
MANNERS & CUSTOMS OF
INDIA. By REV. C. ACLAND. 2s.
ADVENTURES IN MEXICO.
By G. F. RUXTON. 3s. 6d.
PORTUGAL AND GALICIA.
By LORD CARNARVON. 3s. 6d.
BUSH LIFE IN AUSTRALIA.
By REV. H. W. HAYGARTH. 2s.
THE LIBYAN DESERT. By
BAYLE ST. JOHN. 2s.
SIERRA LEONE. By A LADY.
3s. 6d.

*** Each work may be had separately.

HUME (The Student's). A History of England, from the Invasion of Julius Cæsar to the Revolution of 1688. New Edition, revised,
corrected, and continued to the Treaty of Berlin, 1878. By J. S.
BREWER, M.A. With 7 Coloured Maps & 70 Woodcuts. Post 8vo. 7s. 6d.
*** Sold also in 3 parts. Price 2s. 6d. each.

HUNNEWELL (JAMES F.). England's Chronicle in Stone;
Derived from Personal Observations of the Cathedrals, Churches,
Abbeys, Monasteries, Castles, and Palaces, made in Journeys through
the Imperial Island. With Illustrations. Medium 8vo. 24s.

HUTCHINSON (GEN.). Dog Breaking, with Odds and Ends for
those who love the Dog and the Gun. With 40 Illustrations. Crown
8vo. 7s. 6d. *** A Summary of the Rules for Gamekeepers. 1s.

HUTTON (H E.). Principia Græca; an Introduction to the Study
of Greek. Comprehending Grammar, Delectus, and Exercise-book,
with Vocabularies. Sixth Edition. 12mo. 3s. 6d.

HYMNOLOGY, DICTIONARY OF. [See JULIAN.]

ICELAND. [See COLES—DUFFERIN.]

INDIA. [See BROADFOOT—DUFFERIN—ELPHINSTONE—HAND-BOOK
—SMITH—TEMPLE—MONIER WILLIAMS—LYALL.]

IRBY AND MANGLES' Travels in Egypt, Nubia, Syria, and
the Holy Land. Post 8vo. 2s.

JAMES (F. L.). The Wild Tribes of the Soudan : with an account
of the route from Wady Halfa to Dongola and Berber. With
Chapter on the Soudan, by SIR S. BAKER. Illustrations. Crown 8vo.
7s. 6d.

JAMESON (MRS.). Lives of the Early Italian Painters—
and the Progress of Painting in Italy—Cimabue to Bassano. With
50 Portraits. Post 8vo. 12s.

JANNARIS (PROF. A. N.). A Pocket Dictionary of the Modern
Greek and English Languages, as actually Written and Spoken. Being
a copious Vocabulary of all Words and Expressions Current in Ordinary
Reading and in Everyday Talk, with Especial Illustration by means of
Distinctive Signs, of the Colloquial and Popular Greek Language, for
the Guidance of Students and Travellers. Fcap. 8vo.

c

JAPAN. [See BIRD—HANDBOOK—REED.]

JENNINGS (L. J.). Field Paths and Green Lanes : or Walks in Surrey and Sussex. Popular Edition. With Illustrations. Cr. 8vo. 6s. [See also CROKER.]

JERVIS (REV. W. H.). The Gallican Church, from the Concordat of Bologna, 1516, to the Revolution. With an Introduction. Portraits. 2 Vols. 8vo. 28s.

JESSE (EDWARD). Gleanings in Natural History. Fcp. 8vo. 3s. 6d.

JOHNSON'S (DR. SAMUEL) Life. [See BOSWELL.]

JULIAN (REV. JOHN J.). A Dictionary of Hymnology. A Companion to Existing Hymn Books. Setting forth the Origin and History of the Hymns contained in the Principal Hymnals, with Notices of their Authors, &c., &c. Medium 8vo. (1626 pp.) 42s.

JUNIUS' HANDWRITING Professionally investigated. Edited by the Hon. E. TWISLETON. With Facsimiles. Woodcuts, &c. 4to. £3 3s.

KEENE (H. G.). The Literature of France. 220 pp. Crown 8vo. 3s. (University Extension Manuals.)

KENDAL (MRS.) Dramatic Opinions. Post 8vo. 1s.

KERR (ROBT.). The Consulting Architect : Practical Notes on Administrative Difficulties. Crown 8vo. 9s.

KING EDWARD VITH's Latin Grammar. 12mo. 3s. 6d.

——————————— First Latin Book. 12mo. 2s. 6d.

KIRKES' Handbook of Physiology. Edited by W. MORRANT BAKER and V. D. HARRIS. With 500 Illustrations. Post 8vo. 14s.

KNIGHT (PROF.). The Philosophy of the Beautiful. Crown 8vo. 3s. 6d. (University Extension Manuals.)

KUGLER'S HANDBOOK OF PAINTING.—The Italian Schools. A New Edition, revised. By Sir HENRY LAYARD. With 200 Illustrations. 2 vols. Crown 8vo. 30s.

——————————— The German, Flemish, and Dutch Schools. New Edition revised. By Sir J. A. CROWE. With 60 Illustrations. 2 Vols. Crown 8vo. 24s.

LANE (E. W.). Account of the Manners and Customs of Modern Egyptians. With Illustrations. 2 Vols. Post 8vo. 12s.

LAWLESS (HON. EMILY). Major Lawrence, F.L.S. : a Novel. 3 Vols. Crown 8vo. 31s. 6d. Cheap Edition, 6s.

——————————— Plain Frances Mowbray, etc. Crown 8vo. 6s.

LAYARD (Sir A. H.). Nineveh and its Remains. With Illustrations. Post 8vo. 7s. 6d.

——————————— Nineveh and Babylon. Illusts. Post 8vo. 7s. 6d.

——————————— Early Adventures in Persia, Babylonia, and Susiana, including a residence among the Bakhtiyari and other wild tribes, before the discovery of Nineveh. Portrait, Illustrations and Maps. 2 Vols. Crown 8vo. 24s.

LEATHES (STANLEY). Practical Hebrew Grammar. With the Hebrew Text of Genesis i.—vi., and Psalms i.—vi. Grammatical. Analysis and Vocabulary. Post 8vo. 7s. 6d.

LENNEP (REV. H. J. VAN). Travels in Asia Minor. With Illustrations of Biblical History and Archæology. 2 Vols. Post 8vo. 24s.

——————————— Modern Customs and Manners of Bible Lands, in Illustration of Scripture. Illustrations. 2 Vols. 8vo. 21s.

LESLIE (C. R.). Handbook for Young Painters. Illustrations. Post 8vo. 7s. 6d.

LETO (Pomponio). Eight Months at Rome during the Vatican
Council. 8vo. 12s.

LETTERS from the Baltic. By Lady Eastlake. Post 8vo. 2s.

———————— Madras. By Mrs. Maitland. Post 8vo. 2s.

———————— Sierra Leone. By Mrs. Melville. 3s. 6d.

LEVI (Leone). History of British Commerce; and Economic
Progress of the Nation, from 1763 to 1878. 8vo. 18s.

———————— The Wages and Earnings of the Working Classes
in 1888-4. 8vo. 3s. 6d.

LEWIS (T. Hayter). The Holy Places of Jerusalem. Illustrations.
8vo. 10s. 6d.

LEX SALICA; the Ten Texts with the Glosses and the Lex
Emendata. Synoptically edited by J. H. Hessels. With Notes on
the Frankish Words in the Lex Salica by H. Kern, of Leyden. 4to. 42s.

LIDDELL (Dean). Student's History of Rome, from the earliest
Times to the establishment of the Empire. Woodcuts. Post 8vo. 7s. 6d.

LIND (Jenny), The Artist, 1820—1851. Her early Art-life and
Dramatic Career. From Original Documents, Letters, Diaries, &c.,
in the possession of Mr. Goldschmidt. By Canon H. Scott Holland,
M.A., and W. S. Rockstro. With Portraits, Illustrations, and Appendix of Music. 2 Vols. 8vo. 32s.

LINDSAY (Lord). Sketches of the History of Christian Art.
2 Vols. Crown 8vo. 21s.

LISPINGS from LOW LATITUDES; or, the Journal of the Hon.
Impulsia Gushington. Edited by Lord Dufferin. With 24 Plates. 4to. 21s.

LIVINGSTONE (Dr.). First Expedition to Africa, 1840-56.
Illustrations. Post 8vo. 7s. 6d.

———————— Second Expedition to Africa, 1858-64. Illustrations. Post 8vo. 7s. 6d.

———————— Last Journals in Central Africa, to his Death.
By Rev. Horace Waller. Maps and Illustrations. 2 Vols. 8vo. 15s.

———————— Personal Life. By Wm. G. Blaikie, D.D. With
Map and Portrait. 8vo. 6s.

LOCKHART (J. G.). Ancient Spanish Ballads. Historical and
Romantic. Translated, with Notes. Illustrations. Crown 8vo. 5s.

———————— Life of Theodore Hook. Fcap. 8vo. 1s.

LONDON: Past and Present; its History, Associations, and
Traditions. By Henry B. Wheatley, F.S.A. Based on Cunningham's
Handbook. Library Edition, on Laid Paper 3 Vols. Medium 8vo. 3l. 3s.

LOUDON (Mrs.). Gardening for Ladies. With Directions and
Calendar of Operations for Every Month. Woodcuts. Fcap. 8vo. 3s. 6d.

LUMHOLTZ (Dr. C.). Among Cannibals; An Account of Four
Years' Travels in Australia, and of Camp Life among the Aborigines
of Queensland. With Maps and 120 Illustrations. Medium 8vo. 24s.

LUTHER (Martin). The First Principles of the Reformation,
or the Three Primary Works of Dr. Martin Luther. Portrait. 8vo. 12s.

LYALL (Sir Alfred C.), K.C.B. Asiatic Studies; Religious and
Social. 8vo. 12s.

LYELL (Sir Charles). Student's Elements of Geology. A new
Edition, entirely revised by Professor P. M. Duncan, F.R.S. With
(0) Illustrations. Post 8vo. 9s.

———————— Life, Letters, and Journals. Edited by
his sister-in-law, Mrs. Lyell. With Portraits. 2 Vols. 8vo. 30s.

LYNDHURST (Lord). [See Martin.]

McCLINTOCK (Sir L.). Narrative of the Discovery of the Fate of Sir John Franklin and his Companions in the Arctic Seas. With Illustrations. Post 8vo. 7s. 6d.

MACDONALD (A.). Too Late for Gordon and Khartoum. With Maps and Plans. 8vo. 12s.

MACGREGOR (J.). Rob Roy on the Jordan, Nile, Red Sea, Gennesareth, &c. A Canoe Cruise in Palestine and Egypt and the Waters of Damascus. With 70 Illustrations. Crown 8vo. 7s. 6d.

MACKAY (Thomas). The English Poor. A Sketch of their Social and Economic History; and an attempt to estimate the influence of private property on character and habit. Crown 8vo. 7s. 6d.

———— A Flea for Liberty : an Argument against Socialism and Socialistic Legislation. Essays by various Writers. With an Introduction by Herbert Spencer. Third and Popular Edition. With a New and Original Essay on Self Help and State Pensions by C. J. Padley. Post 8vo. 2s.

MAHON (Lord). [See Stanhope.]

MAINE (Sir H. Sumner). A Memoir of, by Sir M. E. Grant Duff, wi h a Selection from his Indian Speeches and Minutes. Edited by Whitley Stokes. With Portrait. 8vo.

———— Ancient Law: its Connection with the Early History of Society, and its Relation to Modern Ideas. 8vo. 9s.

———— Village Communities in the East and West. 8vo. 9s.

———— Early History of Institutions. 8vo. 9s.

———— Dissertations on Early Law and Custom. 8vo. 9s.

———— Popular Government. 8vo. 7s. 6d.

———— International Law. 8vo. 7s. 6d.

MALCOLM (Sir John). Sketches of Persia. Post 8vo. 3s. 6d.

MARCO POLO. [See Yule.]

MARKHAM (Mrs.). History of England. From the First Invasion by the Romans, continued down to 1880. Woodcuts. 12mo. 3s. 6d.

———— History of France. From the Conquest of Gaul by Julius Cæsar, continued down to 1878. Woodcuts. 12mo. 3s. 6d.

———— History of Germany. From its Invasion by Marius to the completion of Cologne Cathedral. Woodcuts. 12mo. 3s. 6d.

———— (Clements R.). A Popular Account of Peruvian Bark and its introduction into British India. With Maps. Post 8vo. 14s.

MARSH (G. P.). Student's Manual of the English Language. Edited with Additions. By Dr. Wm. Smith. Post 8vo. 7s. 6d.

MARTIN (Sir Theodore). Life of Lord Lyndhurst. With Portraits. 8vo. 16s.

MASTERS in English Theology. Lectures by Eminent Divines. With Introduction by Canon Barry. Post 8vo. 7s. 6d.

MATTHIÆ'S Greek Grammar. Abridged by Blomfield. Revised by E. S. Crooke. 12mo. 4s.

MAUREL'S Character, Actions, &c., of Wellington. 1s. 6d.

MELVILLE (Hermann). Marquesas and South Sea Islands. 2 Vols. Post 8vo. 7s.

MEREDITH (Mrs. C.) Notes & Sketches of N. S. Wales. Post 8vo. 2s.

MEXICO. [See Brocklehurst—Ruxton.]

MICHAEL ANGELO, Sculptor, Painter, and Architect. His Life and Works. By C. Heath Wilson. Illustrations. 8vo. 15s.

MILL (Dr. H. R.). The Realm of Nature: An Outline of Physiography. With 19 Coloured Maps and 68 Illustrations and Diagrams (380 pp.). Crown 8vo. 5s. (University Extension Manuals.)

MILLER (Wm.). A Dictionary of English Names of Plants applied among English-speaking People to Plants, Trees, and Shrubs. In Two Parts. Latin-English and English-Latin. Medium 8vo. 12s

MILMAN'S (Dean) WORKS:—
History of the Jews, from the earliest Period down to Modern Times. 3 Vols. Post 8vo. 12s.
Early Christianity, from the Birth of Christ to the Aboli tion of Paganism in the Roman Empire. 3 Vols. Post 8vo. 12s.
Latin Christianity, including that of the Popes to the Pontificate of Nickolas V. 9 Vols. Post 8vo. 36s.
Handbook to St. Paul's Cathedral. Woodcuts. 10s. 6d.
Quinti Horatii Flacci Opera. Woodcuts. Sm. 8vo. 7s. 6d.
Fall of Jerusalem. Fcap. 8vo. 1s.
———— (Bishop, D.D.) Life. With a Selection from his Correspondence and Journals. By his Sister. Map. 8vo. 12s.

MILNE (David, M.A.). A Readable Dictionary of the English Language. Etymologically arranged. Crown 8vo. 7s. 6d.

MINCHIN (J. G.). The Growth of Freedom in the Balkan Peninsula. With a Map. Crown 8vo. 10s. 6d.

MISS BLAKE OF MONKSHALTON. By Isabella Ford. A New Novel. Crown 8vo. 5s.

MIVART (St. George). Lessons from Nature; as manifested in Mind and Matter. 8vo. 15s.

———— The Cat. An Introduction to the Study of Backboned Animals, especially Mammals. With 200 Illustrations. Medium 8vo. 30s.

MOGGRIDGE (M. W.). Method in Almsgiving. A Handbook for Helpers. Post 8vo. 3s. 6d.

MOORE (Thomas). Life and Letters of Lord Byron. [See Byron.]

MORELLI (Giovanni). Italian Painters. Critical Studies of their Works. The Borghese and Doria Pamphili Galleries in Rome. Translated from the German by Constance Jocelyn Ffoulkes, with an Introductory Notice by Sir Henry Layard, G.C.B. 15s.

MOSELEY (Prof. H. N.). Notes by a Naturalist during the voyage of H.M.S. "Challenger" round the World in the years 1872-76, under the command of Captain Sir G. S. Nares and Cap ain F. T. Thom on. A New and Cheaper Edit., with Portrait, Map, and numerous Woodcuts. Crown 8vo.

MOTLEY (John Lothrop). The Correspondence of. With Portrait. 2 Vols. 8vo 30s.

———— History of the United Netherlands: from the Death of William the Silent to the Twelve Years' Truce, 1609. Portraits. 4 Vols. Post 8vo. 6s. each.

———— Life and Death of John of Barneveld. Illustrations. 2 Vols. Post 8vo. 12s.

MUIRHEAD (John H.). The Elements of Ethics. Crown 8vo. 3s. (University Extension Series.)

MUMMERY (A. F.) and J. A. HOBSON. The Physiology of Industry: Being an Exposure of certain Fallacies in existing Theories of Political Economy. Crown 8vo. 6s.

MUNRO'S (General) Life. By Rev. G. R. Gleig. 3s. 6d.

MUNTHE (Axel). Letters from a Mourning City. Naples dur ing the Autumn of 1884. Translated by Maude Valerie White. With a Frontispiece. Crown 8vo. 6s.

MURCHISON (Sir Roderick). And his Contemporaries. By Archibald Geikie. Portraits. 2 Vols. 8vo. 30s.

MURRAY (JOHN). A Publisher and his Friends: Memoir and
Correspondence of the late John Murray, with an Account of the Origin
and Progress of the House, 1768—1843. By SAMUEL SMILES, LL.D.
With Portraits. 2 Vols. 8vo. 32s.

MURRAY (A. S.). A History of Greek Sculpture from the
Earliest Times. With 130 Illustrations. 2 Vols. Medium 8vo. 36s.

———————— Handbook of Greek Archæology. Sculpture,
Vases, Bronzes, Gems, Terra-cottas, Architecture, Mural Paintings,
&c. Many Illustrations. Crown 8vo. 18s.

MURRAY'S MAGAZINE. Vol. I. to Vol. X. 8vo.
7s. 6d. each.

NADAILLAC (MARQUIS DE). Prehistoric America. Translated
by N. D'ANVERS. With Illustrations. 8vo. 16s.

NAPIER (GENERAL SIR CHARLES). His Life. By the Hon.
WM. NAPIER BRUCE. With Portrait and Maps. Crown 8vo. 12s.

———————— (GENERAL SIR GEORGE T.). Passages in his Early
Military Life written by himself. Edited by his Son, GENERAL WM
C. E. NAPIER. With Portrait. Crown 8vo. 7s. 6d.

———————— (SIR WM.). English Battles and Sieges of the Peninsular
War. Portrait. Post 8vo. 5s.

NASMYTH (JAMES). An Autobiography. Edited by Samuel
Smiles, LL.D., with Portrait, and 70 Illustrations. Post 8vo, 6s.; or
Large Paper, 16s.

———————— The Moon: Considered as a Planet, a World, and a
Satellite. With 26 Plates and numerous Woodcuts. Medium 8vo. 21s.

NEWMAN (MRS.). Begun in Jest. A New Novel. 3 vols.
Crown 8vo. 31s. 6d.

NEW TESTAMENT. With Short Explanatory Commentary.
By ARCHDEACON CHURTON, M.A., and the BISHOP OF ST. DAVID'S.
With 110 authentic Views, &c. 2 Vols. Crown 8vo. 21s. bound.

NEWTH (SAMUEL). First Book of Natural Philosophy; an Introduction to the Study of Statics, Dynamics, Hydrostatics, Light, Heat,
and Sound, with numerous Examples. Small 8vo. 3s. 6d.

———————— Elements of Mechanics, including Hydrostatics,
with numerous Examples. Small 8vo. 8s. 6d.

———————— Mathematical Examples. A Graduated Series
of Elementary Examples in Arithmetic, Algebra, Logarithms, Trigo-
nometry, and Mechanics. Small 8vo. 8s. 6d.

NIMROD, On the Chace—Turf—and Road. With Portrait and
Plates. Crown 8vo. 5s. Or with Coloured Plates, 7s. 6d.

NORRIS (W. E.). Marcia. A Novel. Crown 8vo. 6s.

NORTHCOTE'S (SIR JOHN) Notebook in the Long Parliament.
Containing Proceedings during its First Session, 1640. Edited, with
a Memoir, by A. H. A. Hamilton. Crown 8vo. 9s.

OCEAN STEAMSHIPS: A Popular Account of their Construction, Development, Management, and Appliances. By Various Writers.
Beautifully Illustrated, with 96 Woodcuts, Maps, &c. Medium 8vo. 15s.

O'CONNELL (DANIEL). [See FITZPATRICK.]

ORNSBY (PROF. R.). Memoirs of J. Hope Scott, Q.C. (of
Abbotsford). 2 vols. 8vo. 24s.

OTTER (R. H.). Winters Abroad: Some Information respecting
Places visited by the Author on account of his Health. 7s. 6d.

OVID LESSONS. [See ETON.]

OWEN (LIEUT.-COL.). Principles and Practice of Modern Artillery.
With Illustrations. 8vo. 15s.

OXENHAM (REV. W.). English Notes for Latin Elegiacs; with
Prefatory Rules of Composition in Elegiac Metre. 12mo. 3s. 6d.

PAGET (Lord George). The Light Cavalry Brigade in the Crimea. Map. Crown 8vo. 10s. 6d.

PALGRAVE (R. H. I.). Local Taxation of Great Britain and Ireland. 8vo. 5s.

PALLISER (Mrs.). Mottoes for Monuments, or Epitaphs selected for General Use and Study With Illustrations. Crown 8vo. 7s. 6d.

PARKER (C. S.), M.P. [See Peel.]

PEEL'S (Sir Robert) Memoirs. 2 Vols. Post 8vo. 15s.

———— Life of: Early years; as Secretary for Ireland, 1812–18, and Secretary of State, 1822–27. Published by his Trustees, Viscount Hardinge and Right Hon. Arthur Wellesley Peel. Edited by Charles Stuart Parker, M.P. With Portrait. 8vo. 16s.

PENN (Richard). Maxims and Hints for an Angler and Chess-player. Woodcuts. Fcap. 8vo. 1s.

PERCY (John, M.D.). Metallurgy. Fuel, Wood, Peat, Coal, Charcoal, Coke, Fire-Clays. Illustrations. 8vo. 30s.

———— Lead, including part of Silver. Illustrations. 8vo. 30s.

———— Silver and Gold. Part I. Illustrations. 8vo. 30s.

———— Iron and Steel. A New and Revised Edition, with the Author's Latest Corrections, and brought down to the present time. By H. Bauerman, F.G.S. Illustrations. 8vo.

PERRY (Rev. Canon). History of the English Church. See Students' Manuals.

PHILLIPS (Samuel). Literary Essays from "The Times." With Portrait. 2 Vols. Fcap. 8vo. 7s.

POLLOCK (C. E.). A Book of Family Prayers. Selected from the Liturgy of the Church of England. 16mo. 3s. 6d.

POPE'S (Alexander) Life and Works. With Introductions and Notes, by J. W. Croker, Rev. W. Elwin, and W. J. Courthope. 10 Vols. With Portraits. 8vo. 10s. 6d. each.

PORTER (Rev. J. L.). Damascus, Palmyra, and Lebanon. Map and Woodcuts. Post 8vo. 7s. 6d.

PRAYER-BOOK (Beautifully Illustrated). With Notes, by Rev. Thos. James. Medium 8vo. 18s. cloth.

PRINCESS CHARLOTTE OF WALES. Memoir and Correspondence. By Lady Rose Weigall. With Portrait. 8vo. 8s. 6d.

PRITCHARD (Charles, D.D.). Occasional Thoughts of an Astronomer on Nature and Revelation. 8vo. 7s. 6d.

PSALMS OF DAVID. With Notes Explanatory and Critical by Dean Johnson, Canon Elliott, and Canon Cook. Medium 8vo. 10s. 6d.

PUSS IN BOOTS. With 12 Illustrations. By Otto Speckter. 16mo. 1s. 6d. Or coloured, 2s. 6d.

QUARTERLY REVIEW (The). 8vo. 6s.

QUILL (Albert W.). History of P. Cornelius Tacitus. Translated into English, with Introduction and Notes Criti al and Explanatory. 2 Vols. 8vo.

RAE (Edward). Country of the Moors. A Journey from Tripoli to the Holy City of Kairwan. Etchings. Crown 8vo. 12s.

———— The White Sea Peninsula. Journey to the White Sea, and the Kola Peninsula. Illustrations. Crown 8vo. 15s.

———— (George). The Country Banker; His Clients, Cares, and Work, from the Experience of Forty Years. Crown 8vo. 7s. 6d.

RAMSAY (Prof. W. M.). The Historical Geography of Asia Minor. With 6 Maps, Tables, &c. 8vo. 18s.

RASSAM (Hormuzd). British Mission to Abyssinia. Illustrations. 2 Vols. 8vo. 28s.

RAWLINSON'S (Canon) Five Great Monarchies of Chaldæa, Assyria, Media, Babylonia, and Persia. With Maps and Illustrations. 3 Vols. 8vo. 42s.

———— Herodotus, a new English Version. *See* page 12.

RAWLINSON'S (Sir Henry) England and Russia in the East; a Series of Papers on the Condition of Central Asia. Map. 8vo. 12s.

REJECTED ADDRESSES (The). By James and Horace Smith. Woodcuts. Post 8vo. 3s. 6d.; or *Popular Edition*, Fcap. 8vo. 1s.

RICARDO'S (David) Works. With a Notice of his Life and Writings. By J. R. M'Culloch. 8vo. 16s.

RIPA (Father). Residence at the Court of Peking. Post 8vo. 2s.

ROBERTSON (Canon). History of the Christian Church, from the Apostolic Age to the Reformation, 1517. 8 Vols. Post 8vo. 6s. each.

ROBINSON (W.). English Flower Garden. An Illustrated Dictionary of all the Plants used, and Directions for their Culture and Arrangement. With numerous Illustrations. Medium 8vo. 15s.

———— The Vegetable Garden; or, the Edible Vegetables, Salads, and Herbs cultivated in Europe and America. By M. Vilmorin-Andrieux. With 750 Illustrations. 8vo. 15s.

———— Sub-Tropical Garden. Illustrations. Small 8vo. 5s.

———— Parks and Gardens of Paris, considered in Relation to other Cities. 350 Illustrations. 8vo. 18s.

———— Wild Garden; or, Our Groves and Gardens made Beautiful by the Naturalization of Hardy Exotic Plants. With 90 Illustrations. 8vo. 10s. 6d.

———— God's Acre Beautiful; or, the Cemeteries of the Future. With 8 Illustrations. 8vo. 7s. 6d.

ROMANS, St. Paul's Epistle to the. With Notes and Commentary by E. H. Gifford, D.D. Medium 8vo. 7s. 6d.

ROME (History of). [See Gibbon—Inge—Liddell—Smith—Students'.]

ROMILLY (Hugh H.). The Western Pacific and New Guinea. 2nd Edition. With a Map. Crown 8vo. 7s. 6d.

ROSS (Mrs.) The Land of Manfred, Prince of Tarentum and King of Sicily: Rambles in remote parts of S. Italy, with special reference to their Historical associations. Illustrations. Crown 8vo. 10s. 6d.

RUMBOLD (Sir Horace). The Great Silver River: Notes of a Residence in the Argentine Republic. Second Edition, with Additional Chapter. With Illustrations. 8vo. 12s.

RUXTON (Geo. F.). Travels in Mexico; with Adventures among Wild Tribes and Animals of the Prairies and Rocky Mountains. Post 8vo. 3s. 6d.

ST. JOHN (Charles). Wild Sports and Natural History of the Highlands of Scotland. Illustrated Edition. Crown 8vo. 15s. *Cheap Edition*, Post 8vo. 3s. 6d.

———— (Bayle). Adventures in the Libyan Desert. Post 8vo. 2s.

ST. MAUR (Mrs. Algernon), Lady Seymour. Impressions of a Tenderfoot, during a Journey in search of Sport in the Far West. With Map and Illustrations. Crown 8vo. 12s.

SALE'S (Sir Robert) Brigade in Affghanistan. With an Account of the Defence of Jellalabad. By Rev. G. R. Gleig. Post 8vo. 2s.

SALMON (Prof. Geo., D.D.). An Introduction to the Study of the New Testament, and an Investigation into Modern Biblical Criticism, based on the most recent Sources of Information. Crown 8vo. 9s.

———— Lectures on the Infallibility of the Church. Post 8vo. 9s.

SCEPTICISM IN GEOLOGY; and the Reasons for it. An assemblage of facts from Nature combining to refute the theory of "Causes now in Action." By VERIFIER. Woodcuts. Cro 8vo. 6s.

SCHARF (GEORGE). Authentic Portraits of Mary, Queen of Scots. An attempt to distinguish those to be relied upon from others indiscriminately bearing her name, and to dispel the confused ideas that have so long prevailed respecting her personal appearance. With Illustrations. Large 8vo.

SCHLIEMANN (DR. HENRY). Ancient Mycenæ. Illustrations. Medium 8vo. 50s.

———— Ilios; the City and Country of the Trojans, With an Autobiography. Illustrations. Imperial 8vo. 50s.

———— Troja: Results of the Latest Researches and Discoveries on the site of Homer's Troy, and other sites made in 1882. Illustrations. Medium 8vo. 42s.

———— Tiryns: A Prehistoric Palace of the Kings of Tiryns, discovered by excavations in 1884-5. With Illustrations. Medium 8vo. 42s.

SCHREIBER (LADY CHARLOTTE). English Fans and Fan Leaves. Collected and Described. With 160 Plates. Folio. 7l. 7s.

———————————— Foreign Fans and Fan Leaves. French, Italian, and German, chiefly relating to the French Revolution, Collected and Described. 150 Plates. Folio. 7l. 7s.

———————————— Playing Cards of Various Ages and Countries, selec ed from the Collection of Lady Charlotte Schreiber. Vol I., English and Scottish; Dutch and Flemish. With 144 Plates. Folio.

SCOTT (SIR GILBERT). The Rise and Development of Mediæval Architecture. With 400 Illustrations. 2 Vols. Medium 8vo. 42s.

SHAIRP (PRINCIPAL) AND HIS FRIENDS. By Professor WM. KNIGHT, of St. Andrews. With Portrait. 8vo. 15s.

SHAW (T. B.). Manual of English Literature. Post 8vo. 7s. 6d.

———— Specimens of English Literature. Post 8vo. 5s.

———— (ROBERT). Visit to High Tartary, Yarkand, and Kashgar. With Map and Illustrations. 8vo. 16s.

SHAW (R. NORMAN). [See ARCHITECTURE.]

SMILES' (SAMUEL, LL.D.) WORKS:—

BRITISH ENGINEERS; from the Earliest Period to the Death of the Stephensons. Illustrations. 5 Vols. Crown 8vo. 7s. 6d. each.

GEORGE STEPHENSON. Post 8vo. 2s. 6d.

JAMES NASMYTH. Portrait and Illustrations. Post 8vo. 6s.

JASMIN: Barber, Poet, Philanthropist. Post 8vo. 6s.

SCOTCH NATURALIST (THOS. EDWARD). Illustrations. Post 8vo. 6s.

SCOTCH GEOLOGIST (ROBERT DICK). Illustrations. 8vo. 12s.

SELF-HELP. With Illustrations of Conduct and Perseverance. Post 8vo. 6s.

———— In French. 5s.

CHARACTER. A Book of Noble Characteristics. Post 8vo. 6s.

THRIFT. A Book of Domestic Counsel. Post 8vo. 6s.

DUTY. With Illustrations of Courage, Patience, and Endurance. Post 8vo. 6s.

INDUSTRIAL BIOGRAPHY. Iron-Workers and Tool-Makers. 6s.

MEN OF INVENTION. Post 8vo. 6s.

LIFE AND LABOUR; or, Characteristics of Men of Culture and Genius. Post 8vo. 6s.

SMITH'S (SAMUEL, LL.D.) WORKS—_continued._

THE HUGUENOTS; Their Settlements, Churches, and Industries in England and Ireland. Crown 8vo. 7s. 6d.

BOY'S VOYAGE ROUND THE WORLD. Illustrations. Post 8vo. 6s.

SIEMENS (SIR WM.), C.E. Life of. By WM. POLE, C.E. Portraits. 8vo. 16s.

—————— The Scientific Works of: a Collection of Papers and Discourses. Edited by E. F. BAMBER, C.E. Vol. i.—Heat and Metallurgy; ii.—Electricity, &c.; iii.—Addresses and Lectures. Plates. 3 Vols. 8vo. 12s. each.

—————— (DR. WERNER VON). Collected Works of. Translated by E. F. BAMBER. Vol. i.—Scientific Papers and Addresses. ii.—Applied Science. With Illustrations. 8vo.

SIERRA LEONE. By MRS. MELVILLE. Post 8vo. 3s. 6d.

SIMMONS' Constitution and Practice of Courts-Martial. 15s.

SMEDES (SUSAN DABNEY). A Southern Planter. Memoirs of Thomas Dabney. Preface by MR. GLADSTONE. Post 8vo. 7s. 6d.

SMITH (DR. GEORGE) Student's Manual of the Geography of British India, Physical and Political. Maps. Post 8vo. 7s. 6d.

—————— Life of Dr. Somerville of Glasgow, late Evangelist in India, Africa, Australia, Canada, and Chief Countries of Europe (1813-1889). Portrait. Post 8vo. 9s.

—————— Life of Wm. Carey, D.D., 1761—1834. Shoemaker and Missionary. Professor of Sanscrit, Bengalee and Marathee at the College of Fort William, Calcutta. Illustrations. Post 8vo. 7s. 6d.

—————— Life of Stephen Hislop, Pioneer, Missionary, and Naturalist in Central India, 1844-1863. Portrait. Post 8vo. 7s. 6d.

—————— (PHILIP). History of the Ancient World, from the Creation to the Fall of the Roman Empire, A.D. 476. 3 Vols. 8vo. 31s. 6d.

—————— (R. BOSWORTH). Mohammed and Mohammedanism. Crown 8vo. 7s. 6d.

SMITH'S (DR. WM.) DICTIONARIES:—

DICTIONARY OF THE BIBLE; its Antiquities, Biography, Geography, and Natural History. Illustrations. 3 Vols. 8vo. 105s.

CONCISE BIBLE DICTIONARY. Illustrations. 8vo. 21s.

SMALLER BIBLE DICTIONARY. Illustrations. Post 8vo. 7s. 6d.

CHRISTIAN ANTIQUITIES. Comprising the History, Institutions, and Antiquities of the Christian Church. Illustrations. 2 Vols. Medium 8vo. 3l. 13s. 6d.

CHRISTIAN BIOGRAPHY, LITERATURE, SECTS, AND DOCTRINES; from the Times of the Apostles to the Age of Charlemagne. Medium 8vo. Now complete in 4 Vols. 6l. 16s. 6d.

GREEK AND ROMAN ANTIQUITIES. Including the Laws, Institutions, Domestic Usages, Painting, Sculpture, Music, the Drama, &c. Third Edition, Revised and Enlarged. 2 Vols. Med. 8vo. 31s. 6d. each.

GREEK AND ROMAN BIOGRAPHY AND MYTHOLOGY. Illustrations. 3 Vols. Medium 8vo. 4l. 4s.

GREEK AND ROMAN GEOGRAPHY. 2 Vols. Illustrations. Medium 8vo. 56s.

ATLAS OF ANCIENT GEOGRAPHY—BIBLICAL AND CLASSICAL. Folio. 6l. 6s.

CLASSICAL DICTIONARY OF MYTHOLOGY, BIOGRAPHY, AND GEOGRAPHY. 1 Vol. With 750 Woodcuts. 8vo. 18s.

SMALLER CLASSICAL DICT. Woodcuts. Crown 8vo. 7s. 6d.

SMALLER DICTIONARY OF GREEK AND ROMAN ANTIQUITIES. Woodcuts. Crown 8vo. 7s. 6d.

SMALLER LATIN-ENGLISH DICTIONARY. 12mo. 7s. 6d.

SMITH'S (DR. WM.) DICTIONARIES—*continued*.
COMPLETE LATIN-ENGLISH DICTIONARY. With Tables of the
Roman Calendar, Measures, Weights, Money, and a Dictionary of
Proper Names. 8vo. 16s.
COPIOUS AND CRITICAL ENGLISH-LATIN DICT. 8vo. 16s.
SMALLER ENGLISH-LATIN DICTIONARY. 12mo. 7s. 6d.

SMITH'S (DR. WM.) ENGLISH COURSE:—
SCHOOL MANUAL OF ENGLISH GRAMMAR, WITH COPIOUS EXERCISES,
Appendices and Index. Post 8vo. 3s. 6d.
PRIMARY ENGLISH GRAMMAR, for Elementary Schools, with
carefully graduated Parsing Lessons. 16mo. 1s.
MANUAL OF ENGLISH COMPOSITION. With Copious Illustra-
tions and Practical Exercises. 12mo. 3s. 6d.
PRIMARY HISTORY OF BRITAIN. 12mo. 2s. 6d.
SCHOOL MANUAL OF MODERN GEOGRAPHY. Post 8vo. 5s.
A SMALLER MANUAL OF MODERN GEOGRAPHY. 16mo. 2s. 6d.

SMITH'S (DR. WM.) FRENCH COURSE:—
FRENCH PRINCIPIA. Part I. A First Course, containing a
Grammar, Delectus, Exercises, and Vocabularies. 12mo. 3s. 6d.
APPENDIX TO FRENCH PRINCIPIA. Part I. Containing ad-
ditional Exercises, with Examination Papers. 12mo. 2s. 6d.
FRENCH PRINCIPIA. Part II. A Reading Book, containing
Fables, Stories, and Anecdotes, Natural History, and Scenes from the
History of France. With Grammatical Questions, Notes and copious
Etymological Dictionary. 12mo. 4s. 6d.
FRENCH PRINCIPIA. Part III. Prose Composition, containing
Hints on Translation of English into French, the Principal Rules of
the French Syntax compared with the English, and a Systematic Course
of Exercises on the Syntax. 12mo. 4s. 6d. [Post 8vo. 6s.
STUDENT'S FRENCH GRAMMAR. With Introduction by M. Littré.
SMALLER GRAMMAR OF THE FRENCH LANGUAGE. Abridged
from the above. 12mo. 3s. 6d.

SMITH'S (DR. WM.) GERMAN COURSE:—
GERMAN PRINCIPIA. Part I. A First German Course, contain-
ing a Grammar, Delectus, Exercise Book, and Vocabularies. 12mo. 3s. 6d.
GERMAN PRINCIPIA. Part II. A Reading Book ; containing
Fables, Anecdotes, Natural History, and Scenes from the History of
Germany. With Questions, Notes, and Dictionary. 12mo. 3s. 6d.
PRACTICAL GERMAN GRAMMAR. Post 8vo. 3s. 6d.

SMITH'S (DR. WM.) ITALIAN COURSE:—
ITALIAN PRINCIPIA. Part I. An Italian Course, containing a
Grammar, Delectus, Exercise Book, with Vocabularies, and Materials
for Italian Conversation. 12mo. 3s. 6d.
ITALIAN PRINCIPIA. Part II. A First Italian Reading Book,
containing Fables, Anecdotes, History, and Passages from the best
Italian Authors, with Grammatical Questions, Notes, and a Copious
Etymological Dictionary. 12mo. 3s. 6d. [Children].

SMITH'S (DR. WM.) YOUNG BEGINNER'S FIRST LATIN COURSE (for
I. A FIRST LATIN BOOK. The Rudiments of Grammar, Easy
Grammatical Questions and Exercises with Vocabularies. 12mo. 2s.
II. A SECOND LATIN BOOK. An Easy Latin Reading Book,
with an Analysis of the Sentences, Notes, and a Dictionary. 12mo. 2s.
III. A THIRD LATIN BOOK. The Principal Rules of Syntax,
with Easy Exercises, Questions, Vocabularies, and an English-Latin
Dictionary. 2s.
IV. A FOURTH LATIN BOOK. A Latin Vocabulary for Beginners.
Arranged according to Subjects and Etymologies. 12mo. 2s.

SMITH'S (Dr. Wm.) LATIN COURSE.

PRINCIPIA LATINA. Part I. First Latin Course, containing a Grammar, Delectus, and Exercise Book, with Vocabularies. 12mo. 3s. 6d.

. In this Edition the Cases of the Nouns, Adjectives, and Pronouns are arranged both as in the ORDINARY GRAMMARS and as in the PUBLIC SCHOOL PRIMER, together with the corresponding Exercises.

APPENDIX TO PRINCIPIA LATINA. Part I.; being Additional Exercises, with Examination Papers. 12mo. 2s. 6d.

PRINCIPIA LATINA. Part II. A Reading-book of Mythology, Geography, Roman Antiquities, and History. With Notes and Dictionary. 12mo. 3s. 6d.

PRINCIPIA LATINA. Part III. A Poetry Book. Hexameters and Pentameters; Eclog. Ovidianæ; Latin Prosody. 12mo. 3s. 6d.

PRINCIPIA LATINA. Part IV. Prose Composition. Rules of Syntax, with Examples, Explanations of Synonyms, and Exercises on the Syntax. 12mo. 3s. 6d.

PRINCIPIA LATINA. Part V. Short Tales and Anecdotes for Translation into Latin. A New and Enlarged Edition. 12mo. 3s. 6d.

LATIN-ENGLISH VOCABULARY AND FIRST LATIN-ENGLISH DICTIONARY FOR PILÆDRUS, CORNELIUS NEPOS, AND CÆSAR. 12mo. 3s. 6d.

STUDENT'S LATIN GRAMMAR. For the Higher Forms. A new and thoroughly revised Edition. Post 8vo. 6s.

SMALLER LATIN GRAMMAR. New Edition. 12mo. 3s. 6d.

SMITH'S (Dr. Wm.) GREEK COURSE:—

INITIA GRÆCA. Part I. A First Greek Course, containing a Grammar, Delectus, and Exercise-book. With Vocabularies. 12mo. 3s. 6d.

APPENDIX TO INITIA GRÆCA. Part I. Containing additional Exercises. With Examination Papers. Post 8vo. 2s. 6d.

INITIA GRÆCA. Part II. A Reading Book. Containing Short Tales, Anecdotes, Fables, Mythology, and Grecian History. 12mo. 3s. 6d.

INITIA GRÆCA. Part III. Prose Composition. Containing the Rules of Syntax, with copious Examples and Exercises. 12mo. 3s. 6d.

STUDENT'S GREEK GRAMMAR. For the Higher Forms. Post 8vo. 6s.

SMALLER GREEK GRAMMAR. 12mo. 3s. 6d.

GREEK ACCIDENCE. 12mo. 2s. 6d.

PLATO, Apology of Socrates, &c. With Notes. 12mo. 3s. 6d.

SMITH'S (Dr. Wm.) SMALLER HISTORIES:—

SCRIPTURE HISTORY. Maps and Woodcuts. 16mo. 3s. 6d.

ANCIENT HISTORY. Woodcuts. 16mo. 3s. 6d.

ANCIENT GEOGRAPHY. Woodcuts. 16mo. 3s. 6d.

MODERN GEOGRAPHY. 16mo. 2s. 6d.

GREECE. With Coloured Map and Woodcuts. 16mo. 3s. 6d.

ROME. With Coloured Maps and Woodcuts. 16mo. 3s. 6d.

CLASSICAL MYTHOLOGY. Woodcuts. 16mo. 3s. 6d.

ENGLAND. With Coloured Maps and Woodcuts. 16mo. 3s. 6d.

ENGLISH LITERATURE. 16mo. 3s. 6d.

SPECIMENS OF ENGLISH LITERATURE. 16mo. 3s. 6d.

SOMERVILLE (MARY). Physical Geography. Post 8vo. 9s.

———— Connexion of the Physical Sciences. Post 8vo. 9s.

———— (DR., OF GLASGOW). [See SMITH, GEORGE.]

SOUTH (John F.). Household Surgery; or, Hints for Emergen-
cies. With Woodcuts. Fcap. 8vo. 3s. 6d.

SOUTHEY (Robt.). Lives of Bunyan and Cromwell. Post 8vo. 2s.

STANHOPE'S (Earl) WORKS:—
HISTORY OF ENGLAND FROM THE REIGN OF QUEEN ANNE TO
THE PEACE OF VERSAILLES, 1701-83. 9 Vols. Post 8vo. 5s. each.
LIFE OF WILLIAM PITT. Portraits. 3 Vols. 8vo. 36s.
NOTES OF CONVERSATIONS WITH THE DUKE OF WELLINGTON.
Crown 8vo. 7s. 6d.
MISCELLANIES. 2 Vols. Post 8vo. 13s.
BRITISH INDIA, FROM ITS ORIGIN TO 1783. Post 8vo. 3s. 6d.
HISTORY OF "FORTY-FIVE." Post 8vo. 3s.
HISTORICAL AND CRITICAL ESSAYS. Post 8vo. 3s. 6d.
RETREAT FROM MOSCOW, AND OTHER ESSAYS. Post 8vo. 7s. 6d.
LIFE OF CONDÉ. Post 8vo. 3s. 6d.
STORY OF JOAN OF ARC. Fcap. 8vo. 1s.
ADDRESSES ON VARIOUS OCCASIONS. 16mo. 1s.
[See also WELLINGTON.]

STANLEY'S (Dean) WORKS:—
SINAI AND PALESTINE. Coloured Maps. 8vo. 12s.
BIBLE IN THE HOLY LAND; Extracts from the above Work.
Woodcuts. Post 8vo. 3s. 6d.
EASTERN CHURCH. Plans. Crown 8vo. 6s.
JEWISH CHURCH. From the Earliest Times to the Christian
Era. Portrait and Maps. 3 Vols. Crown 8vo. 18s.
CHURCH OF SCOTLAND. 8vo. 7s. 6d.
EPISTLES OF ST. PAUL TO THE CORINTHIANS. 8vo. 18s.
LIFE OF DR. ARNOLD. Portrait. 2 Vols. Cr. 8vo. 12s.
CANTERBURY. Illustrations. Crown 8vo. 6s.
WESTMINSTER ABBEY. Illustrations. 8vo. 15s.
SERMONS PREACHED IN WESTMINSTER ABBEY. 8vo. 12s.
MEMOIR OF EDWARD, CATHERINE, AND MARY STANLEY. Cr. 8vo. 9s.
CHRISTIAN INSTITUTIONS. Crown 8vo. 6s.
ESSAYS ON CHURCH AND STATE: 1850—1870. Crown 8vo. 6s.
SERMONS TO CHILDREN, including the Beatitudes, the Faithful
Servant, &c. Post 8vo. 3s. 6d.
[See also BRADLEY.]

STEBBING (Wm.). Some Verdicts of History Reviewed. 8vo. 12s.

STEPHENS (Rev. W. R. W.). Life and Times of St. John
Chrysostom. A Sketch of the Church and the Empire in the Fourth
Century. Portrait. 8vo. 7s. 6d.

STREET (G. E.), R.A. Gothic Architecture in Brick and Marble.
With Notes on North of Italy. Illustrations. Royal 8vo. 26s.
——— Memoir of. By ARTHUR E. STREET. Portrait. 8vo. 15s.

STUART (Villiers). Egypt after the War. With Descriptions of
the Homes and Habits of the Natives, &c. Coloured Illustrations
and Woodcuts. Royal 8vo. 31s. 6d
——————— Adventures Amidst the Equatorial Forests and
Rivers of South America, also in the West Indies and the Wilds of
Florida; to which is added "Jamaica Revisited." With Map and
Illustrations. Royal 8vo. 21s.

STUDENTS' MANUALS. Post 8vo. 7s. 6d. each Volume:—

Hume's History of England from the Invasion of Julius Cæsar to the Revolution in 1688. Revised, and continued to the Treaty of Berlin, 1878. By J. S. Brewer, M.A. Coloured Maps and Woodcuts. Or in 3 parts, price 2s. 6d. each.
*** Questions on the above Work, 12mo. 2s.

History of Modern Europe, from the Fall of Constantinople to the Treaty of Berlin, 1878. By R. Lodge, M.A.

Old Testament History; from the Creation to the Return of the Jews from Captivity. Woodcuts.

New Testament History. With an Introduction connecting the History of the Old and New Testaments. Woodcuts.

Evidences of Christianity. By H. Wace, D.D. [In the Press.

Ecclesiastical History; a History of the Christian Church. By Philip Smith, B.A. With numerous Woodcuts. 2 Vols. Part I. A.D. 30—1003. Part II., 1003—1614.

English Church History. By Canon Perry. 3 Vols. First Period, A.D. 596—1509. Second Period, 1509—1717. Third Period, 1717—1834.

Ancient History of the East; Egypt, Assyria, Babylonia, Media, Persia, Asia Minor, and Phœnicia. By Philip Smith, B.A. Woodcuts.

——— Geography. By Canon Bevan. Woodcuts.

History of Greece; from the Earliest Times to the Roman Conquest. By Wm. Smith, D.C.L. Woodcuts.
*** Questions on the above Work, 12mo. 2s.

History of Rome; from the Earliest Times to the Establishment of the Empire. By Dean Liddell. Woodcuts.

History of the Roman Empire; from the Establishment of the Empire to the reign of Commodus. By J. B. Bury. With 1 Illustrations.

Gibbon's Decline and Fall of the Roman Empire. Woodcuts.

Hallam's History of Europe during the Middle Ages.

Hallam's History of England; from the Accession of Henry VII. to the Death of George II.

History of France; from the Earliest Times to the Fall of the Second Empire. By H. W. Jervis. With Coloured Maps and Woodcuts.

English Language. By Geo. P. Marsh.

English Literature. By T. B. Shaw, M.A.

Specimens of English Literature. By T. B. Shaw. 5s.

Modern Geography; Mathematical, Physical and Descriptive. By Canon Bevan, M A. Woodcuts.

Geography of British India. Political and Physical. By George Smith, LL.D. Maps.

Moral Philosophy. By Wm. Fleming.

STURGIS (Julian). Comedy of a Country House. 6s.

SUMNER'S (Bishop) Life and Episcopate during 40 Years. By Rev. G. H. Sumner. Portrait. 8vo. 14s.

SWAINSON (Canon). Nicene and Apostles' Creeds; Their Literary History; together with some Account of "The Creed of St. Athanasius." 8vo. 16s.

TACITUS. [See Quill.]

TEMPLE (Sir Richard). India in 1880. With Maps. 8vo. 16s.

——— Men and Events of My Time in India. 8vo. 16s.

TEMPLE (Sir Richard). Oriental Experience. Essays and
Addresses delivered on Various Occasions. With Maps and Woodcuts. 8vo. 16s.

THIBAUT'S (Antoine) Purity in Musical Art. With Prefatory
Memoir by W. H. Gladstone, M.P. Post 8vo. 7s. 6d.

THOMAS (Sidney Gilchrist), Inventor; Memoir and Letters.
Edited by R. W. Burnie. Portraits. Crown 8vo. 9s.

THOMSON (J. Arthur). The Study of Animal Life. With many
Illustrations. (University Extension Manuals.)

THORNHILL (Mark). The Personal Adventures and Experiences
of a Magistrate during the Indian Mutiny. Crown 8vo. 12s.

TITIAN'S LIFE AND TIMES. By Crowe and Cavalcaselle.
Illustrations. 2 Vols. 8vo. 21s.

TOCQUEVILLE'S State of Society in France before the Revolution,
1789, and on the Causes which led to that Event. 8vo. 12s.

TOZER (Rev. H. F.). Highlands of Turkey, with Visits to Mounts
Ida, Athos, Olympus, and Pelion. 2 Vols. Crown 8vo. 24s.

———— Lectures on the Geography of Greece. Post 8vo. 9s.

TRISTRAM (Canon). Great Sahara. Illustrations. Crown 8vo. 15s.

———— Land of Moab : Travels and Discoveries on the East
Side of the Dead Sea and the Jordan. Illustrations. Crown 8vo. 15s.

TWINING (Rev. Thos.). Recreations and Studies of a Country
Clergyman of the Last Century. 2 Vols. Crown 8vo. 9s. each.

———— (Louisa). Symbols and Emblems of Early and
Mediæval Christian Art. With 500 Illustrations. Crown 8vo. 6s.

TYLOR (E. B.). Researches into the Early History of Mankind,
and Development of Civilization. 3rd Edition. 8vo. 12s.

———— Primitive Culture: the Development of Mythology,
Philosophy, Religion. Art, and Custom. 2 Vols. 8vo. 3rd Edit. 21s.

UNIVERSITY EXTENSION MANUALS. Edited by Professor Wm. Knight (St. Andrew's). A series of Manuals dealing
with Literature, Science, Philosophy, History, Art, &c. Crown 8vo.
Prospectus with full particulars will be forwarded on application.

VIRCHOW (Professor). The Freedom of Science in the
Modern State. Fcap. 8vo. 2s.

WACE (Rev. Henry), D.D. The Principal Facts in the Life of
our Lord, and the Authority of the Evangelical Narratives. Post 8vo. 6s.

———— Christianity and Morality. Boyle Lectures for 1874 and
1875. Seventh Edition. Crown 8vo. 6s.

———— The Foundations of Faith, being the Bampton Lectures
for 1879. 8vo. 7s. 6d.

WALES (H.R.H. the Prince of). Speeches and Addresses.
1863-1888. Edited by Dr. J. Macaulay. With Portrait. 8vo. 12s.

WELLINGTON (Duke of). Notes of Conversations with the
late Earl Stanhope. 1831-1851. Crown 8vo. 7s. 6d.

———— Supplementary Despatches, relating to India,
Ireland, Denmark, Spanish America, Spain, Portugal, France, Congress
of Vienna, Waterloo and Paris. 15 Vols. 8vo. 20s. each.

———— Civil and Political Correspondence. Vols. I. to
VIII. 8vo. 20s.

————Speeches in Parliament. 2 Vols. 8vo. 42s.

WESTCOTT (Canon B. F.) The Gospel according to St. John, with
Notes and Dissertations (Reprinted from the Speaker's Commentary.)
8vo. 10s. 6d.

WHARTON (Capt. W. J. L.), R.N. Hydrographical Surveying :
being a description of the means and methods employed in constructing
Marine Charts. With Illustrations. 8vo. 15s.

WHITE (W. H.). Manual of Naval Architecture, for the use of N val Officers, Shipbuilders, and Yachtsmen, &c. Illustrations. 8vo. 24s.

WHYMPER (EDWARD). Travels amongst the Great Andes of the Equator. With 140 Original Illustrations, drawn by F. BARNARD. A. CORBOULD, F. DADD, W. E. LAPWORTH, W. H. OVEREND, P. SKELTON, E. WAGNER, E. WILSON, JOSEPH WOLF, and others. Engraved by the Author. With Maps and Illustrations. Medium 8vo. 21s. Net. To range with "Scrambles amongst the Alps."

———— Supplementary Appendix to the above. With 61 Figures of New Genera and Species. Illus. Medium 8vo. 21s. Net.

———— How to Use the Aneroid Barometer. With numerous Tables. 2s. 6d. Net.

WILBERFORCE'S (BISHOP) Life of William Wilberforce. Portrait. Crown 8vo. 6s.

———— (SAMUEL, D.D.), Lord Bishop of Oxford and Winchester; his Life. By CANON ASHWELL, and R. G. WILBERFORCE. Portraits. 3 Vols. 8vo. 15s. each.

WILKINSON (SIR J. G.). Manners and Customs of the Ancient Egyptians, their Private Life, Laws, Arts, Religion, &c. A new edition. Edited by SAMUEL BIRCH, LL.D. Illustrations. 3 Vols. 8vo. 84s.

————Popular Account of the Ancient Egyptians. With 500 Woodcuts. 2 Vols. Post 8v . 12s.

WILLIAMS (SIR MONIER). Brahmanism and Hinduism, Religious Thought and Life in India as based on the Veda. Enlarged Edit. 18s.

———— Buddhism; its connection with Brahmanism and Hinduism, and in its contrast with Christianity. With Illus. 8vo. 21s.

WINTLE (H. G.). Ovid Lessons. 12mo, 2s. 6d. [See ETON.]

WOOD'S (CAPTAIN) Source of the Oxus. With the Geography of the Valley of the Oxus. By COL. YULE. Map. 8vo. 12s.

WOODS (MRS.). Esther Vanhomrigh. A Novel. Crown 8vo. 6s.

WORDS OF HUMAN WISDOM. Collected and Arranged by E. S. With a Preface by CANON LIDDON. Fcap. 8vo. 3s. 6d.

WORDSWORTH (BISHOP). Greece; Pictorial, Descriptive, and Historical. With an Introduction n the Characteristics of Greek Art, by GEO. SCHARF. New Edition revised by the Rev. H. F. TOZER, M.A. With 400 Illustrations. Royal 8vo. 31s. 6d.

———— (CHARLES), Bishop of St. Andrews. The Collects of the Church of England, together with certain Psalms and Hymns appropriate to the Principal Festivals, rendered into Latin Verse. Crown 8vo, gilt edges, 5s.

YORK (ARCHBISHOP OF). Collected Essays. Crown 8vo. 9s.

YORK-GATE LIBRARY (Catalogue of). Formed by Mr. SILVER. An Index to the Literature of Geography, Maritime and Inland Discovery, Commerce and Colonisation. Compiled by E. A. PETHERICK. 2nd Edition. Royal 8vo. 42s.

YOUNGHUSBAND (CAPT. G. J.). The Queen's Commission: How to Prepare for it; how to Obtain it, and how to Use it. With Practical Information on the Cost and Prospects of a Military Career. Intended for Cadets, Subalterns, and Parents. Crown 8vo. 6s.

YULE (COLONEL). The Book of Ser Marco Polo, the Venetian, concerning the Kingdoms and Marvels of the East. Illustrated by the Light of Oriental Writers and Modern Travels. With Maps and 80 Plates. 2 Vols. Medium 8vo.

———— and A. C. BURNELL. A Glossary of Anglo-Indian Colloquial Words and Phrases, and of Kindred Terms; Etymological, Historical, Geographical, and Discursive. Medium 8vo. 36s.

———— (A. F.). The Cretan Insurrection. Post 8vo. 2s. 6d.

BRADBURY, AGNEW, & CO. LD., PRINTERS, WHITEFRIARS.